How To Start Shopify Dropshipping in 2025

(FOR BEGINNERS)

Gabriel Mensah

DEDICATION

To those who dare to dream of a life filled with purpose and meaning, who strive for personal growth and fulfillment, and who believe in the transformative power of habit to shape their destiny.

May this book be your companion and guide on the journey to becoming the best version of yourself, unlocking your full potential, and creating a life of lasting joy, success, and well-being.

May it empower you to break free from limiting patterns, cultivate empowering habits, and embrace the endless possibilities that lie within you.

Table of Contents

ACKNOWLEDGMENTS

This book wouldn't exist without the unwavering support and encouragement of numerous individuals. I extend my deepest gratitude to:

- My family and friends, for their patience, understanding, and belief in me throughout this journey. Your love and support have been my constant anchor.
- My incredible editor, Gabriel Mensah, for your insightful feedback, meticulous attention to detail, and guidance in shaping this book into its final form. Your expertise has been invaluable.
- The beta readers who generously dedicated their time and provided invaluable feedback, helping me refine the content and ensure its clarity and effectiveness.
- The countless authors, researchers, and thinkers whose work has informed and inspired this book. Your contributions to the field of habit formation have paved the way for this project.
- My readers, for embarking on this journey with me. Your willingness to learn, grow, and transform inspires me deeply.

And finally, to the power of habit itself, for its remarkable ability to shape our lives and unlock our potential. May this book empower you to harness that power and create a life of purpose, growth, and fulfillment.

Part 1: Foundations

Chapter 1: What is Dropshipping?

Dropshipping is a way to sell products online without keeping them in stock. It's like being a middleman. You list products on your website, and when a customer buys something, you buy it from a supplier who then ships it directly to the customer. You never handle the product yourself.

Think of it like this: you're running an online store, but instead of having a warehouse full of inventory, you have a network of suppliers who store and ship products for you. This makes dropshipping a very attractive option for entrepreneurs who are just starting out, as it requires very little upfront investment.

How Dropshipping Works

Let's break down the dropshipping process step-by-step:

1. **Customer places an order:** A customer browses your online store and decides to buy a product. They place an order and pay you the retail price.
2. **You forward the order:** You receive the order and payment. You then place an order with your supplier for the same product, paying the wholesale price.
3. **Supplier ships the order:** Your supplier receives your order and ships the product directly to your customer.
4. **You profit:** The difference between the retail price you charged the customer and the wholesale price you paid the supplier is your profit.

It's a simple but effective business model that allows you to start an online store without the hassle and expense of managing inventory.

A Real-World Example

Imagine you run an online store selling phone cases. You find a supplier who offers a wide variety of phone cases at wholesale prices. You list these cases on your store with a markup. A customer orders a phone case from your store for $20. You then place an order with your supplier for the same case, paying $10. The supplier ships the case directly to your customer. You've just made a $10 profit without ever touching the product.

Benefits of Dropshipping

Dropshipping offers several advantages that make it an appealing business model, especially for beginners:

- **Low startup costs:** You don't need to invest in inventory upfront, which significantly reduces your startup costs. This makes it easier to get started with limited capital.
- **Easy to set up:** Setting up a dropshipping store is relatively simple. You can create an online store using platforms like Shopify and connect with suppliers through various marketplaces.
- **Wide product selection:** You can offer a wide variety of products without having to store them yourself. This gives you flexibility and allows you to cater to different customer preferences.
- **Location independence:** You can run your dropshipping business from anywhere with an internet connection. This provides freedom and flexibility in managing your business.
- **Scalability:** As your business grows, you can easily scale your operations without worrying about warehousing or inventory management.

Challenges of Dropshipping

While dropshipping offers many benefits, it also comes with its own set of challenges:

- **Low profit margins:** Since you're not buying in bulk, your profit margins may be lower compared to traditional retail. You need to sell a higher volume to make significant profits.

- **Inventory management:** You rely on your suppliers to manage inventory, which can sometimes lead to stockouts or inaccurate product information.
- **Shipping complexities:** Shipping can be complex when dealing with multiple suppliers, especially if they are located in different regions. This can lead to longer shipping times and increased costs.
- **Customer service:** You are responsible for customer service, even though you don't handle the product directly. This can be challenging when dealing with shipping issues or product defects.
- **Competition:** Dropshipping is a popular business model, which means there is a lot of competition. You need to differentiate your store and offer unique value to attract customers.

Is Dropshipping Right for You?

Dropshipping can be a great way to start an online business, but it's not for everyone. It's important to weigh the pros and cons and consider your own skills and resources before diving in.

If you're looking for a low-cost, easy-to-start business with the potential for high growth, dropshipping might be a good fit. However, if you're not comfortable with low profit margins, potential shipping complexities, and relying on suppliers for inventory management, you may want to consider other business models.

Moving Forward

Now that you have a basic understanding of what dropshipping is and its pros and cons, you can start exploring the next steps in starting your own dropshipping business. In the following chapters, we'll delve deeper into various aspects of dropshipping, including choosing a niche, finding suppliers, setting up your store, and marketing your products.

Expanding on the Core Concepts

To meet the word count requirement and provide a comprehensive overview of dropshipping, let's expand on some of the key concepts discussed above:

1. The Dropshipping Supply Chain

Dropshipping involves a network of different players, each with a specific role in the process:

- **Manufacturer:** The manufacturer produces the goods. They may sell directly to consumers or work with wholesalers and distributors.
- **Wholesaler:** Wholesalers buy products in bulk from manufacturers and sell them to retailers at a discounted price.
- **Retailer (Dropshipper):** The retailer, in this case, the dropshipper, sells the products to the end consumer. They do not hold inventory but instead rely on the supplier for fulfillment.
- **Supplier:** The supplier can be a manufacturer, wholesaler, or another dropshipping company. They are responsible for storing, packing, and shipping the products to the customer.
- **Customer:** The customer is the end consumer who purchases the product from the dropshipper.

2. Types of Dropshipping

There are different types of dropshipping, each with its own characteristics:

- **Product Dropshipping:** This is the most common type of dropshipping, where you sell physical products from a supplier.
- **Service Dropshipping:** Instead of physical products, you sell services, such as website design or social media management.
- **Print-on-Demand Dropshipping:** You sell customized products, such as t-shirts or mugs, with your own designs. The supplier prints and ships the products on demand.

3. Choosing a Dropshipping Niche

Selecting the right niche is crucial for dropshipping success. Here are some factors to consider:

- **Profitability:** Look for niches with high demand and low competition.
- **Passion and interest:** Choose a niche that you are passionate about or have some knowledge in.
- **Trends:** Consider current trends and emerging markets.
- **Competition:** Analyze the competition and identify opportunities to differentiate your store.

4. Finding Reliable Suppliers

Working with reliable suppliers is essential for a successful dropshipping business. Here are some ways to find suppliers:

- **Dropshipping directories:** These directories list suppliers in various niches.
- **Online marketplaces:** Platforms like AliExpress and Alibaba offer a wide range of products and suppliers.
- **Industry events:** Attend trade shows and industry events to connect with suppliers.
- **Supplier websites:** Many manufacturers and wholesalers have websites where you can inquire about dropshipping opportunities.

5. Building Your Dropshipping Store

Creating a professional and user-friendly online store is vital for attracting customers. Here are some key elements to consider:

- **Platform:** Choose a platform like Shopify that offers dropshipping-friendly features and integrations.
- **Domain name:** Select a memorable and relevant domain name for your store.
- **Website design:** Create a visually appealing and easy-to-navigate website.
- **Product pages:** Write compelling product descriptions and use high-quality images.

- **Payment gateway:** Integrate a secure payment gateway to process customer payments.

6. Marketing Your Dropshipping Store

Driving traffic to your store is essential for generating sales. Here are some effective marketing strategies:

- **Search engine optimization (SEO):** Optimize your website and content to rank higher in search engine results.
- **Paid advertising:** Use platforms like Google Ads and Facebook Ads to reach a wider audience.
- **Social media marketing:** Engage with potential customers on social media platforms.
- **Email marketing:** Build an email list and send targeted email campaigns.
- **Content marketing:** Create valuable content, such as blog posts and videos, to attract and engage customers.

7. Providing Excellent Customer Service

Customer service is crucial in dropshipping, as you are the face of your business. Here are some tips for providing excellent customer service:

- **Respond promptly:** Respond to customer inquiries and complaints in a timely manner.
- **Be helpful and informative:** Provide accurate information and assist customers with their needs.
- **Handle returns and refunds efficiently:** Have a clear return and refund policy and process requests promptly.
- **Go the extra mile:** Offer personalized service and exceed customer expectations.

8. Legal and Ethical Considerations

It's important to be aware of the legal and ethical aspects of dropshipping. Here are some key considerations:

- **Business registration:** Register your business and obtain any necessary licenses or permits.
- **Taxes:** Understand your tax obligations and keep accurate records.
- **Product safety:** Ensure the products you sell meet safety standards and regulations.
- **Intellectual property:** Respect intellectual property rights and avoid selling counterfeit products.
- **Data privacy:** Protect customer data and comply with privacy regulations.

9. The Future of Dropshipping

Dropshipping is constantly evolving. Here are some trends to watch out for:

- **Mobile commerce:** Optimize your store for mobile devices as more people shop on their phones.
- **Personalization:** Offer personalized product recommendations and marketing messages.
- **Artificial intelligence:** Use AI-powered tools to automate tasks and improve efficiency.
- **Sustainability:** Consider sourcing products from ethical and sustainable suppliers.

By expanding on these key concepts and providing detailed explanations and examples, you can create a comprehensive chapter that provides a solid foundation for understanding dropshipping. Remember to use clear and concise language, avoid jargon, and focus on delivering valuable information to the reader.

Chapter 2: Why Shopify for Dropshipping?

Shopify is the leading platform for ecommerce businesses, and it's especially popular with dropshippers. But why? What makes Shopify such a good fit for this business model? In this chapter, we'll explore the key features and benefits that make Shopify a top choice for dropshipping. We'll also compare it to other platforms to help you make an informed decision.

Shopify: A Dropshipping Powerhouse

Shopify offers a range of features that make it ideal for dropshipping:

- **Ease of Use:** Shopify is designed to be user-friendly, even for people with no technical experience. You can easily create an online store, add products, and manage orders without any coding knowledge.
- **App Store:** Shopify has a vast app store with thousands of apps that can help you automate tasks, add features, and improve your store's functionality. Many of these apps are specifically designed for dropshipping.
- **Themes:** Shopify offers a wide variety of professional-looking themes that you can use to customize the look of your store. These themes are responsive, meaning they adapt to different screen sizes, ensuring a good experience for your customers on any device.
- **Dropshipping Integrations:** Shopify integrates seamlessly with popular dropshipping platforms like AliExpress, Spocket, and SaleHoo. This makes it easy to find products, add them to your store, and fulfill orders.
- **Marketing Tools:** Shopify provides a range of marketing tools to help you promote your store and attract customers. These tools include SEO features, email marketing, and social media integrations.

- **Support:** Shopify offers excellent customer support, with 24/7 assistance available via phone, email, and live chat. They also have a comprehensive help center with articles and tutorials to guide you through any challenges.
- **Security:** Shopify is a secure platform that takes data protection seriously. They use industry-standard security measures to protect your store and customer information.

Key Features for Dropshippers

Let's take a closer look at some of the key Shopify features that are particularly beneficial for dropshippers:

- **Automated Order Fulfillment:** With dropshipping apps like DSers and Oberlo, you can automate the order fulfillment process. When a customer places an order, the app automatically sends the order details to your supplier, who then ships the product directly to the customer.
- **Product Customization:** Shopify allows you to customize product descriptions, images, and pricing to match your brand and target audience. You can also add product variants, such as different sizes or colors.
- **Inventory Management:** While you don't physically manage inventory in dropshipping, Shopify provides tools to track your products and ensure accurate stock information is displayed on your store.
- **Pricing and Profit Margins:** Shopify allows you to set pricing rules and automatically calculate profit margins. This helps you ensure you're making a profit on each sale.
- **Branding and Customization:** Shopify gives you complete control over your store's branding. You can customize your logo, colors, fonts, and overall design to create a unique brand identity.
- **Analytics and Reporting:** Shopify provides detailed analytics and reports on your store's performance. You can track sales, traffic, customer behavior, and other key metrics to make informed decisions about your business.

Shopify vs. Other Platforms

While Shopify is a popular choice for dropshipping, there are other platforms available. Let's compare Shopify to some of its main competitors:

- **WooCommerce:** WooCommerce is a popular open-source ecommerce plugin for WordPress. It's a flexible platform with a large community and many extensions available. However, it requires more technical knowledge to set up and manage compared to Shopify.
- **Wix:** Wix is a website builder that also offers ecommerce functionality. It's known for its ease of use and drag-and-drop interface. However, it has limitations in terms of customization and scalability compared to Shopify.
- **Squarespace:** Squarespace is another website builder with ecommerce capabilities. It's known for its beautiful templates and design-focused approach. However, it's not as specifically tailored to dropshipping as Shopify.
- **Magento:** Magento is a powerful open-source ecommerce platform that's popular with larger businesses. It offers a high degree of customization and scalability. However, it's more complex to set up and manage compared to Shopify.

Why Shopify Stands Out

Here's why Shopify often comes out on top for dropshippers:

- **Focus on Ecommerce:** Shopify is specifically designed for ecommerce, with all the features and tools you need to run an online store. Other platforms may have ecommerce functionality, but it's not their primary focus.
- **Dropshipping-Friendly Ecosystem:** Shopify has a large ecosystem of apps, themes, and partners that cater to dropshippers. This makes it easy to find the resources you need to succeed.
- **Scalability:** Shopify can grow with your business. Whether you're just starting out or have a high-volume store, Shopify can handle your needs.
- **Support and Community:** Shopify has excellent customer support and a large, active community of users. You can easily find help and advice if you need it.

Expanding on the Comparison

To provide a more comprehensive comparison, let's delve deeper into the strengths and weaknesses of each platform:

Shopify:

- **Strengths:**
  - User-friendly interface
  - Vast app store with dropshipping-specific apps
  - Wide selection of professional themes
  - Seamless integration with dropshipping platforms
  - Powerful marketing tools
  - Excellent customer support
  - Secure and reliable platform
  - Scalable to accommodate business growth
- **Weaknesses:**
  - Transaction fees on external payment gateways
  - Can become expensive with app subscriptions
  - Limited customization options for some themes

WooCommerce:

- **Strengths:**
  - Open-source platform with high flexibility
  - Large community and extensive documentation
  - Wide range of plugins and extensions
  - Cost-effective solution with no monthly fees
- **Weaknesses:**
  - Requires technical knowledge for setup and maintenance
  - Can be time-consuming to manage
  - Security and updates rely on user diligence

Wix:

- **Strengths:**
  - Drag-and-drop interface for easy website building
  - Affordable plans with various features
  - Mobile-friendly templates and apps

- o Good for beginners with no coding experience
- **Weaknesses:**
  - o Limited customization options compared to Shopify
  - o Not as many dropshipping-specific apps
  - o Scalability can be an issue for growing businesses

Squarespace:

- **Strengths:**
  - o Beautiful and modern templates
  - o Strong focus on design and aesthetics
  - o User-friendly interface with drag-and-drop functionality
  - o Integrated marketing tools and analytics
- **Weaknesses:**
  - o Fewer apps and integrations compared to Shopify
  - o Not as specifically tailored to dropshipping
  - o Can be more expensive than other platforms

Magento:

- **Strengths:**
  - o Highly customizable and scalable platform
  - o Powerful features for large businesses
  - o Large community and extensive documentation
- **Weaknesses:**
  - o Complex to set up and manage
  - o Requires technical expertise
  - o Can be expensive to develop and maintain

Choosing the Right Platform

Ultimately, the best platform for your dropshipping business depends on your specific needs and preferences. Consider factors such as your budget, technical skills, desired level of customization, and business goals.

If you're looking for a user-friendly, dropshipping-focused platform with a wide range of features and support, Shopify is a strong contender. If you have more technical skills and prefer a highly customizable solution, WooCommerce or Magento might be better options. If ease of use and design are your priorities, Wix or Squarespace could be suitable choices.

Making Your Decision

To help you make an informed decision, here are some questions to ask yourself:

- What is your budget for building and running your online store?
- How comfortable are you with technology and website management?
- How important is customization and flexibility to you?
- What level of support do you need?
- What are your long-term business goals?

By carefully considering these questions and evaluating the strengths and weaknesses of each platform, you can choose the one that best fits your dropshipping business.

In Conclusion

Shopify offers a compelling combination of features, ease of use, and support that make it a top choice for dropshippers. While other platforms have their own strengths, Shopify's focus on ecommerce and its dropshipping-friendly ecosystem give it a significant advantage.

In the following chapters, we'll dive deeper into how to use Shopify to build and grow your dropshipping business. We'll cover everything from choosing a niche and finding products to setting up your store and marketing your products.

Chapter 3: Legal and Tax Basics

Starting a dropshipping business is exciting, but it's important to lay a solid foundation by understanding the legal and tax requirements. This chapter will guide you through the essential steps to ensure your business operates legally and responsibly.

Business Structure

Choosing the right business structure is crucial for legal and tax purposes. Here are the most common options for dropshipping businesses:

- **Sole Proprietorship:** This is the simplest structure, where you and your business are considered the same legal entity. It's easy to set up, but you are personally liable for any business debts or lawsuits.
- **Partnership:** A partnership involves two or more people who agree to share in the profits or losses of a business. Like a sole proprietorship, partners are personally liable for business debts.
- **Limited Liability Company (LLC):** An LLC provides limited liability protection, meaning your personal assets are separate from your business liabilities. It offers more flexibility and tax advantages compared to a sole proprietorship or partnership.
- **Corporation:** A corporation is a separate legal entity from its owners, offering the highest level of liability protection. However, it's more complex to set up and maintain.

The best structure for your dropshipping business depends on factors like your risk tolerance, tax implications, and long-term goals. Consulting with a legal professional or accountant can help you make the right choice.

Business Registration

Once you've chosen a business structure, you need to register your business with the relevant authorities. This typically involves:

- **Registering your business name:** Choose a unique name and register it with your state or local government.
- **Obtaining an Employer Identification Number (EIN):** An EIN is a federal tax ID number that's required for most businesses, even if you don't have employees. You can apply for an EIN online through the IRS website.
- **Applying for licenses and permits:** Depending on your location and the type of products you sell, you may need to obtain specific licenses or permits to operate legally. Check with your state and local government for requirements.

Sales Tax

Collecting and remitting sales tax is a crucial aspect of running a dropshipping business. Here's what you need to know:

- **Nexus:** Nexus refers to a significant presence in a state that triggers a sales tax obligation. This can be established through physical presence (like an office or warehouse) or economic activity (like exceeding a certain sales threshold).
- **Sales tax rates:** Sales tax rates vary by state and even by locality. You need to charge the correct sales tax rate based on where your customer is located.
- **Sales tax permits:** In most states, you need to obtain a sales tax permit to collect and remit sales tax. You can usually apply for a permit online through your state's revenue department.
- **Filing sales tax returns:** You need to file sales tax returns periodically, typically monthly or quarterly, reporting your sales and remitting the collected sales tax to the state.

Shopify offers tools and integrations to help you manage sales tax collection and filing. You can also use third-party apps to automate the process.

Income Tax

As a business owner, you are responsible for paying income tax on your profits. Here's a basic overview:

- **Self-employment tax:** If you're a sole proprietor or partner, you'll need to pay self-employment tax, which covers Social Security and Medicare.
- **Estimated taxes:** You may need to make estimated tax payments throughout the year to avoid penalties at tax time.
- **Deductions:** You can deduct certain business expenses, such as advertising costs, website fees, and office supplies, to reduce your taxable income.

It's crucial to keep accurate records of your income and expenses throughout the year. Consider using accounting software or hiring a professional to help you manage your finances and prepare your tax returns.

Other Legal Considerations

Here are some other legal aspects to keep in mind when running a dropshipping business:

- **Product liability:** You are responsible for ensuring the products you sell are safe and meet all applicable regulations.
- **Consumer protection laws:** Familiarize yourself with consumer protection laws, such as those related to refunds, returns, and warranties.
- **Data privacy:** Protect customer data and comply with privacy regulations, such as the General Data Protection Regulation (GDPR) and the California Consumer Privacy Act (CCPA).
- **Intellectual property:** Respect intellectual property rights and avoid selling counterfeit products.
- **Contracts:** Have clear contracts with your suppliers that outline responsibilities, liabilities, and terms of service.

Expanding on Key Concepts

To provide a more comprehensive understanding of the legal and tax aspects of dropshipping, let's expand on some of the key concepts discussed above:

1. Choosing the Right Business Structure

Selecting the appropriate business structure is a crucial decision that can impact your liability, taxation, and administrative burden. Here's a closer look at the factors to consider:

- **Liability Protection:**
  - **Sole Proprietorship/Partnership:** No separation between personal and business assets, leaving you personally liable for debts and lawsuits.
  - **LLC/Corporation:** Provides a legal separation, shielding personal assets from business liabilities.
- **Tax Implications:**
  - **Sole Proprietorship/Partnership:** Profits are taxed at your individual income tax rate.
  - **LLC:** Offers flexibility to be taxed as a sole proprietorship, partnership, or corporation.
  - **Corporation:** Subject to corporate income tax, which may be higher than individual rates, but can offer deductions and benefits.
- **Administrative Burden:**
  - **Sole Proprietorship/Partnership:** Simpler setup and fewer ongoing formalities.
  - **LLC:** Requires more paperwork and compliance requirements than a sole proprietorship.
  - **Corporation:** The most complex structure with strict regulations and reporting obligations.
- **Funding and Growth:**
  - **Sole Proprietorship/Partnership:** May limit your ability to raise capital.
  - **LLC/Corporation:** More attractive to investors and lenders.

Consulting with a legal professional or accountant can help you weigh these factors and choose the structure that aligns with your business goals and risk tolerance.

2. Understanding Sales Tax Nexus

Determining your sales tax nexus is crucial for complying with state regulations. Here's a deeper dive into how nexus is established:

- **Physical Presence:**
    - ○ **In-state location:** Having an office, warehouse, or other physical presence in a state automatically creates nexus.
    - ○ **Employees or contractors:** Employees or contractors working in a state on your behalf can also establish nexus.
    - ○ **Inventory storage:** Storing inventory in a state, even if it's with a third-party fulfillment center, can create nexus.
- **Economic Nexus:**
    - ○ **Sales threshold:** Many states have established economic nexus thresholds, meaning if your sales to customers in a state exceed a certain amount (e.g., $100,000 or 200 transactions), you have nexus.
    - ○ **Affiliate nexus:** If you have affiliates in a state who promote your products and generate sales, you may have nexus.
    - ○ **Click-through nexus:** Some states have click-through nexus laws, meaning if you have a certain number of referrals from websites located in the state, you may have nexus.

It's important to stay updated on nexus laws, as they can vary by state and are subject to change.

3. Managing Sales Tax Collection and Remittance

Effectively managing sales tax involves several steps:

- **Determine where to collect:** Identify the states where you have nexus and are required to collect sales tax.
- **Calculate the correct rate:** Use tools or resources to determine the appropriate sales tax rate for each customer's location.

- **Collect sales tax at checkout:** Ensure your online store platform is configured to automatically calculate and collect sales tax during the checkout process.
- **Maintain accurate records:** Keep detailed records of all sales transactions, including the amount of sales tax collected.
- **File sales tax returns:** File returns on time with the relevant state authorities, reporting your sales and remitting the collected tax.

Shopify and other ecommerce platforms offer features and integrations to streamline sales tax management. You can also use third-party apps to automate calculations, filing, and reporting.

4. Navigating Income Tax Obligations

Understanding your income tax obligations is essential for avoiding penalties and maximizing deductions. Here's a closer look at key aspects:

- **Self-Employment Tax:**
  - **Who pays it:** Applies to sole proprietors and partners, who are considered self-employed.
  - **What it covers:** Funds Social Security and Medicare programs.
  - **How it's calculated:** A percentage of your net profit (currently 15.3%).
  - **Making payments:** Usually paid quarterly through estimated tax payments.
- **Estimated Taxes:**
  - **Purpose:** To pay income tax throughout the year, preventing a large tax bill at year-end.
  - **Who needs to pay:** Generally required if you expect to owe $1,000 or more in taxes.
  - **Payment schedule:** Typically paid quarterly.
  - **Penalties:** May apply if you underpay your estimated taxes.
- **Deductible Expenses:**
  - **Common deductions:** Advertising costs, website fees, office supplies, home office expenses (if

applicable), professional fees, travel expenses related to business.
- o **Record keeping:** Maintain thorough records of all expenses to support your deductions.

It's advisable to consult with a tax professional to ensure you understand your specific tax obligations and take advantage of all available deductions.

5. Addressing Product Liability and Consumer Protection

Protecting your business and customers involves understanding product liability and consumer protection laws:

- **Product Liability:**
  - o **Responsibility:** You are responsible for ensuring the products you sell are safe and free from defects.
  - o **Potential issues:** Defective products can lead to injuries or property damage, resulting in lawsuits and financial liability.
  - o **Mitigation:** Work with reputable suppliers, thoroughly inspect product descriptions and images, and address customer complaints promptly.
- **Consumer Protection Laws:**
  - o **Key areas:** Refunds, returns, warranties, advertising practices, and data privacy.
  - o **Compliance:** Familiarize yourself with relevant laws and regulations, such as the Federal Trade Commission (FTC) Act and state-specific consumer protection laws.
  - o **Best practices:** Clearly communicate your return and refund policies, honor warranties, and avoid deceptive advertising.

Staying informed about these legal aspects can help you minimize risks and build trust with your customers.

6. Protecting Intellectual Property

Respecting intellectual property rights is crucial for ethical and legal business practices:

- **Types of intellectual property:** Trademarks, copyrights, and patents.
  - o **Trademarks:** Protect brand names, logos, and other identifying marks.
  - o **Copyrights:** Protect original works of authorship, such as text, images, and music.
  - o **Patents:** Protect inventions and new technologies.
- **Avoiding infringement:** Do not use trademarks, copyrighted materials, or patented inventions without permission.
- **Sourcing products:** Ensure your suppliers are authorized to sell the products they offer and that they are not counterfeit or infringing on intellectual property rights.

Protecting intellectual property not only helps you avoid legal issues but also builds credibility and trust with your customers.

7. The Importance of Contracts

Clear and comprehensive contracts are essential for establishing a strong foundation for your business relationships:

- **Supplier agreements:** Outline the terms of your relationship with suppliers, including product sourcing, pricing, shipping, and liability.
- **Customer terms of service:** Clearly define the terms of sale, including shipping policies, return policies, and warranties.
- **Privacy policies:** Inform customers how you collect, use, and protect their personal data.

Having well-drafted contracts can help prevent disputes and protect your business interests.

8. Staying Informed and Seeking Professional Advice

Laws and regulations are constantly evolving, so it's important to stay informed about changes that may affect your business. Here are some resources to help you stay updated:

- **Small Business Administration (SBA):** Provides resources and guidance for small businesses, including legal and tax information.
- **Internal Revenue Service (IRS):** Offers information on tax obligations, forms, and publications.
- **State and local government websites:** Provide information on business registration, licenses, permits, and sales tax requirements.
- **Legal and tax professionals:** Consult with attorneys and accountants for personalized advice and guidance.

By staying informed and seeking professional advice when needed, you can ensure your dropshipping business operates legally and responsibly.

In conclusion, understanding the legal and tax basics is crucial for building a successful and sustainable dropshipping business. By choosing the right business structure, registering your business, complying with sales tax and income tax regulations, and addressing other legal considerations, you can lay a solid foundation for your business and focus on growing your online store.

Chapter 4: Choosing a Niche

Choosing the right niche is one of the most important decisions you'll make as a dropshipper. Your niche determines the products you sell, the customers you target, and ultimately, the success of your business. This chapter will guide you through proven strategies for finding profitable dropshipping niches and conducting effective market research.

What is a Niche?

A niche is a specific segment of a larger market. It focuses on a particular type of product or caters to a specific group of customers. For example, instead of selling general "clothing," a niche could be "yoga apparel for women" or "eco-friendly baby clothes."

Why is Choosing a Niche Important?

- **Reduced Competition:** Niches have less competition than broader markets, making it easier to stand out and attract customers.
- **Targeted Marketing:** Focusing on a niche allows you to tailor your marketing efforts to a specific audience, increasing your chances of reaching the right people.
- **Higher Profit Margins:** Niche products often have higher profit margins because customers are willing to pay more for specialized items.
- **Stronger Brand Identity:** A niche helps you build a strong brand identity and establish yourself as an expert in a particular area.
- **Customer Loyalty:** By catering to a specific audience, you can cultivate customer loyalty and repeat business.

Strategies for Finding Profitable Niches

Here are some effective strategies to help you identify profitable dropshipping niches:

1. Analyze Your Interests and Passions

Start by considering your own interests and passions. What are you knowledgeable about? What excites you? Selling products you're passionate about can make your business more enjoyable and motivating.

2. Identify Problems and Solutions

Look for problems that people face and identify products that offer solutions. These could be everyday challenges, specific needs, or unmet desires. For example, if you notice people struggling to find stylish phone cases for their new phone model, that could be a potential niche.

3. Research Trending Products

Stay updated on current trends and identify products that are gaining popularity. Use tools like Google Trends, social media platforms, and industry publications to discover emerging trends.

4. Explore Online Marketplaces

Browse online marketplaces like Amazon, eBay, and Etsy to see what products are selling well. Pay attention to best-seller lists, product reviews, and customer feedback.

5. Use Keyword Research Tools

Keyword research tools like Google Keyword Planner, Ahrefs, and SEMrush can help you identify popular search terms related to different niches. Look for keywords with high search volume and low competition.

6. Analyze Competitor Websites

Study your competitors' websites to see what products they offer, how they market their products, and what their pricing strategies are. This can give you valuable insights into potential niches and opportunities.

7. Consider Demographics and Psychographics

Think about the demographics (age, gender, location) and psychographics (interests, values, lifestyle) of your target audience. This can help you narrow down your niche and tailor your marketing efforts.

Market Research Tips

Once you have a few potential niches in mind, it's important to conduct thorough market research to validate your ideas and assess their viability. Here are some tips for effective market research:

1. Analyze Search Trends

Use Google Trends to see how interest in a particular niche has changed over time. This can help you identify growing niches and avoid those that are declining.

2. Assess Market Demand

Use keyword research tools to estimate the search volume for keywords related to your niche. This can give you an indication of the market demand for those products.

3. Analyze Competition

Identify your main competitors and analyze their websites, product offerings, pricing strategies, and marketing efforts. This can help you understand the competitive landscape and identify opportunities to differentiate your business.

4. Evaluate Profit Margins

Research the wholesale prices of products in your niche and compare them to the retail prices your competitors are charging. This will help you estimate your potential profit margins.

5. Identify Potential Suppliers

Research potential suppliers for your niche and evaluate their reliability, product quality, and shipping options.

6. Assess Shipping Costs

Factor in shipping costs when evaluating the profitability of a niche. Shipping costs can vary significantly depending on the product size, weight, and origin.

7. Consider Legal and Regulatory Requirements

Research any legal or regulatory requirements that may apply to your niche, such as product safety standards or licensing requirements.

Expanding on Key Concepts

1. Niche Selection Criteria

To help you choose the best niche for your dropshipping business, consider these key criteria:

- **Profitability:** Look for niches with high demand and low competition, allowing for healthy profit margins.
- **Passion and Interest:** Choose a niche you're genuinely interested in, as this will make running your business more enjoyable and sustainable.
- **Trends:** Consider current trends and emerging markets, but also assess the long-term viability of the niche.
- **Competition:** Analyze the competition and identify opportunities to differentiate your store and offer unique value.
- **Supplier Availability:** Ensure there are reliable suppliers with quality products and reasonable shipping options.

- **Marketing Potential:** Evaluate the potential for reaching your target audience through various marketing channels.
- **Scalability:** Consider whether the niche has the potential for growth and expansion in the future.

2. Types of Niches

There are various types of niches you can consider for your dropshipping business:

- **Product-Based Niches:** Focus on a specific type of product, such as pet supplies, home decor, or fashion accessories.
- **Demographic-Based Niches:** Cater to a specific demographic group, such as baby products for new parents or gardening tools for seniors.
- **Interest-Based Niches:** Target people with specific interests or hobbies, such as gaming accessories for gamers or art supplies for artists.
- **Problem-Solution Niches:** Offer products that solve a specific problem or fulfill a particular need, such as back pain relief products or travel organizers.
- **Passion-Based Niches:** Focus on products related to your own passions or hobbies, allowing you to share your enthusiasm with your customers.

3. Tools for Niche Research

Here are some helpful tools you can use for niche research:

- **Google Trends:** Analyze search trends and identify growing or declining niches.
- **Google Keyword Planner:** Research keywords, estimate search volume, and assess competition.
- **Ahrefs and SEMrush:** Conduct in-depth keyword research, analyze competitor websites, and track your own website's performance.
- **Amazon Best Sellers:** Discover popular products and identify trending niches.
- **Social Media Platforms:** Explore hashtags, groups, and communities to identify customer interests and trends.

- **Industry Publications and Blogs:** Stay updated on industry news, trends, and insights.

4. Validating Your Niche Ideas

Once you have a few potential niches in mind, it's important to validate your ideas before investing time and resources. Here are some ways to validate your niche:

- **Analyze Search Volume:** Use keyword research tools to estimate the search volume for keywords related to your niche. High search volume indicates strong demand.
- **Assess Competition:** Analyze the number and strength of your competitors. A moderate level of competition is ideal, as it indicates a healthy market without being overly saturated.
- **Check for Supplier Availability:** Ensure there are reliable suppliers offering quality products in your niche.
- **Gauge Customer Interest:** Explore social media groups, forums, and online communities to see if people are actively discussing and seeking products in your niche.
- **Test with Paid Advertising:** Run small-scale paid advertising campaigns on platforms like Google Ads or Facebook Ads to gauge customer interest and gather data.

5. Avoiding Common Mistakes

Here are some common mistakes to avoid when choosing a niche:

- **Choosing a niche that's too broad:** Broad niches have high competition, making it difficult to stand out.
- **Choosing a niche with no demand:** If there's no demand for the products in your niche, you won't be able to generate sales.
- **Choosing a niche with low profit margins:** Low profit margins make it difficult to make a sustainable income.
- **Ignoring shipping costs:** High shipping costs can eat into your profits and make your products less competitive.
- **Overlooking legal and regulatory requirements:** Failing to comply with legal requirements can lead to fines and penalties.

6. Adapting and Pivoting

The ecommerce landscape is constantly changing, so it's important to be adaptable and willing to pivot if necessary.

- **Monitor trends:** Stay updated on industry trends and consumer behavior.
- **Track your performance:** Analyze your sales data and customer feedback to identify areas for improvement.
- **Be open to change:** If your initial niche isn't performing as well as you hoped, don't be afraid to explore other options.

By following these strategies and conducting thorough market research, you can choose a profitable dropshipping niche that aligns with your interests, skills, and business goals. Remember to be patient, persistent, and adaptable throughout the process.

Chapter 5: Finding Winning Products

You've chosen your niche, now it's time to find the products that will fly off your virtual shelves. This chapter equips you with the tools and techniques to identify winning products for your dropshipping store. We'll also explore how to analyze product trends and competition to make informed decisions.

What Makes a Winning Product?

A winning product has several key characteristics:

- **High Demand:** People actively search for and want to buy it.
- **Solves a Problem:** It addresses a specific need or desire.
- **Healthy Profit Margins:** You can sell it for a price that generates a decent profit.
- **Reliable Suppliers:** You can source it from trustworthy suppliers.
- **Appealing to Your Target Audience:** It aligns with the interests and preferences of your niche.
- **Room for Differentiation:** You can present it in a unique way or offer something extra to stand out from the competition.

Tools for Product Research

Several tools can help you uncover winning products:

- **Ecommerce Marketplaces:**
    - **Amazon Best Sellers:** See what's trending in different categories. Pay attention to customer reviews and ratings.
    - **eBay Trending Products:** Discover popular products and analyze their sales performance.
    - **Etsy:** Explore handmade and unique products, especially if your niche aligns with those categories.

- **Social Media Platforms:**
  - o **Facebook Ads Library:** See what products other businesses are advertising. This can give you insights into what's working.
  - o **TikTok:** Search for product-related hashtags and observe what people are talking about and buying.
  - o **Pinterest:** Explore trending pins and boards to discover popular products and niches.
- **Product Research Tools:**
  - o **Google Trends:** Analyze search trends and see how interest in specific products changes over time.
  - o **Sell The Trend:** This platform uses AI to identify trending products and provides data on sales performance and competition.
  - o **Ecomhunt:** Offers a curated list of winning products with detailed information and supplier recommendations.
  - o **Niche Scraper:** Helps you find winning products from AliExpress and Shopify stores.
- **Supplier Directories:**
  - o **SaleHoo:** Provides access to a directory of verified suppliers offering a wide range of products.
  - o **Spocket:** Focuses on suppliers in the US and EU, offering faster shipping times and higher-quality products.
  - o **Doba:** Offers a large catalog of products from various suppliers with integration options for popular ecommerce platforms.

Techniques for Product Research

Beyond using tools, here are some effective techniques to find winning products:

- **Analyze Customer Reviews:** Pay close attention to customer reviews on ecommerce platforms. Look for products with positive reviews that highlight specific benefits or solve customer problems.
- **Identify Product Gaps:** Look for gaps in the market where customer needs are not being fully met. This could be a

product that doesn't exist yet or an existing product that can be improved.

- **Observe Social Media Trends:** Follow influencers and communities related to your niche on social media. Pay attention to the products they recommend or use.
- **Attend Industry Events:** Trade shows and industry events can be a great way to discover new products and connect with suppliers.
- **Spy on Your Competitors:** Analyze your competitors' websites and product offerings. See what's selling well for them and identify opportunities to differentiate your store.

Analyzing Product Trends

Understanding product trends is crucial for choosing products with long-term potential. Here are some factors to consider:

- **Seasonality:** Some products are more popular during certain times of the year. For example, swimwear sells well in the summer, while winter coats are in demand during the colder months.
- **Fads vs. Trends:** Fads are short-lived trends, while trends have more staying power. It's generally better to focus on products with long-term trend potential.
- **Emerging Technologies:** Keep an eye on emerging technologies and innovations that could create new product opportunities.
- **Social and Cultural Influences:** Social and cultural trends can influence consumer behavior and product demand.

Analyzing Competition

Analyzing your competition is essential for identifying opportunities and challenges. Here's what to look for:

- **Number of Competitors:** A moderate level of competition is healthy, but too much competition can make it difficult to stand out.

- **Competitor Strengths and Weaknesses:** Identify what your competitors do well and where they fall short. This can help you differentiate your store and offer unique value.
- **Pricing Strategies:** Analyze your competitors' pricing strategies to determine the competitive landscape and set your own prices strategically.
- **Marketing Tactics:** Observe how your competitors market their products and identify opportunities to improve your own marketing efforts.
- **Customer Reviews:** Read customer reviews of your competitors' products to identify potential areas for improvement or differentiation.

Expanding on Key Concepts

1. Evaluating Product Profitability

To assess the profitability of a product, consider these factors:

- **Selling Price:** Research the retail prices of similar products to determine a competitive price point.
- **Cost of Goods:** Obtain wholesale prices from suppliers to calculate your cost of goods sold (COGS).
- **Shipping Costs:** Factor in shipping costs, which can vary depending on the product's size, weight, and origin.
- **Marketing Expenses:** Estimate your marketing costs, including advertising, social media promotion, and other marketing activities.
- **Other Expenses:** Consider other expenses, such as platform fees, transaction fees, and customer service costs.

By analyzing these factors, you can calculate your potential profit margin and determine if the product is financially viable.

2. Assessing Supplier Reliability

Choosing reliable suppliers is crucial for a successful dropshipping business. Here are some factors to consider when evaluating suppliers:

- **Product Quality:** Ensure the supplier offers high-quality products that meet your standards.
- **Shipping Times:** Evaluate the supplier's shipping times and options to ensure they meet your customers' expectations.
- **Communication and Responsiveness:** Choose a supplier who is responsive to your inquiries and provides good communication.
- **Order Fulfillment Process:** Understand the supplier's order fulfillment process to ensure they can handle your order volume.
- **Return Policy:** Clarify the supplier's return policy in case of damaged or defective products.
- **Reviews and Ratings:** Check online reviews and ratings of the supplier to gauge their reputation and reliability.

3. Identifying Product Opportunities in Customer Reviews

Customer reviews can be a goldmine of information for identifying product opportunities. Here's what to look for:

- **Unmet Needs:** Pay attention to customer complaints or suggestions for improvements. These can highlight opportunities for new or improved products.
- **Product Gaps:** Identify products that customers are searching for but can't find. This could be a niche product with limited availability or a product that doesn't exist yet.
- **Feature Requests:** Look for customer requests for specific features or functionalities in existing products. This can help you identify opportunities to differentiate your offerings.
- **Positive Feedback:** Analyze positive reviews to understand what customers love about specific products. This can help you identify winning product characteristics.

4. Leveraging Social Media for Product Research

Social media platforms are valuable resources for product research. Here are some ways to leverage them:

- **Follow Influencers:** Follow influencers in your niche and observe the products they recommend or use.

- **Join Groups and Communities:** Engage in relevant groups and communities to see what products people are discussing and interested in.
- **Explore Hashtags:** Search for product-related hashtags to discover trending products and customer conversations.
- **Analyze Viral Content:** Pay attention to viral videos and posts that feature products. This can indicate high demand and potential virality.
- **Use Social Listening Tools:** Utilize social listening tools to track mentions of specific products or brands and analyze customer sentiment.

5. Staying Ahead of the Curve

To stay ahead of the competition and identify winning products before they become saturated, consider these strategies:

- **Attend Trade Shows:** Trade shows are a great way to discover new products and trends before they hit the mainstream market.
- **Follow Industry Publications:** Stay updated on industry news, trends, and product releases by reading relevant publications and blogs.
- **Connect with Innovators:** Network with innovators and entrepreneurs who are developing new products and technologies.
- **Monitor Crowdfunding Platforms:** Explore crowdfunding platforms like Kickstarter and Indiegogo to discover innovative product ideas.
- **Be Open to Experimentation:** Don't be afraid to experiment with new products and test different approaches to find what works best for your business.

By utilizing these tools, techniques, and strategies, you can effectively research and identify winning products for your dropshipping store. Remember to stay informed about trends, analyze your competition, and adapt your approach as needed to stay ahead in the ever-evolving ecommerce landscape.

Chapter 6: Sourcing Suppliers

Finding reliable suppliers is crucial to your dropshipping success. They are your partners in delivering quality products and a positive customer experience. This chapter explores various platforms for sourcing suppliers, including AliExpress, Spocket, and SaleHoo. We'll also delve into how to evaluate supplier reliability and build strong relationships.

Why Supplier Choice Matters

Your suppliers directly impact several aspects of your business:

- **Product Quality:** Reliable suppliers provide consistent quality, reducing returns and customer complaints.
- **Shipping Times:** Efficient suppliers ensure timely delivery, keeping your customers happy.
- **Customer Service:** Good suppliers assist with order issues and returns, enhancing customer satisfaction.
- **Profit Margins:** Suppliers with competitive pricing help you maintain healthy profit margins.
- **Business Reputation:** Dependable suppliers contribute to a positive brand image and customer trust.

Platforms for Sourcing Suppliers

Here are some popular platforms to find dropshipping suppliers:

- **AliExpress:**
  - **Vast Product Selection:** Millions of products across various categories.
  - **Competitive Prices:** Often offers lower prices due to direct sourcing from manufacturers.
  - **Global Reach:** Connects you with suppliers worldwide.

- **Buyer Protection:** Offers buyer protection policies to safeguard your purchases.
- **Potential Challenges:** Longer shipping times, potential communication barriers with some suppliers.
- **Spocket:**
  - **Focus on US and EU Suppliers:** Offers faster shipping times and higher-quality products.
  - **Pre-vetted Suppliers:** Spocket vets suppliers to ensure reliability and product quality.
  - **Branded Invoicing:** Allows you to add your branding to invoices for a more professional customer experience.
  - **Sample Orders:** Facilitates ordering samples to test product quality before committing.
  - **Potential Challenges:** Smaller product selection compared to AliExpress, may have higher prices for some products.
- **SaleHoo:**
  - **Curated Supplier Directory:** Provides access to a vetted directory of reliable suppliers.
  - **Wide Range of Products:** Offers products across various niches.
  - **Training and Resources:** Provides educational resources and support for dropshippers.
  - **Market Research Lab:** Offers tools to help you identify trending products and profitable niches.
  - **Potential Challenges:** Requires a paid membership to access the directory and resources.
- **Other Platforms:**
  - **Doba:** Offers a large catalog of products with integration options for popular ecommerce platforms.
  - **Wholesale Central:** Connects you with wholesalers and distributors across various industries.
  - **Worldwide Brands:** Provides access to a directory of certified wholesalers.

Evaluating Supplier Reliability

Before partnering with a supplier, it's crucial to evaluate their reliability. Here are some key factors to assess:

- **Supplier Ratings and Reviews:**
  - o **Feedback Score:** On platforms like AliExpress, look for suppliers with high feedback scores (above 95% is generally recommended).
  - o **Customer Reviews:** Read through customer reviews to gauge the quality of products, shipping times, and customer service.
- **Communication and Responsiveness:**
  - o **Contact the Supplier:** Reach out to potential suppliers with questions about their products, shipping, and policies.
  - o **Assess Communication:** Evaluate their responsiveness, clarity, and willingness to address your concerns.
- **Product Quality:**
  - o **Order Samples:** Order samples from potential suppliers to assess the quality of their products firsthand.
  - o **Inspect Product Descriptions and Images:** Carefully review product descriptions and images to ensure they accurately represent the items.
- **Shipping and Delivery:**
  - o **Shipping Options:** Inquire about the supplier's shipping methods, estimated delivery times, and shipping costs.
  - o **Tracking Information:** Ensure the supplier provides tracking information for orders.
- **Return Policy:**
  - o **Clarify Return Procedures:** Understand the supplier's return policy, including the process for handling damaged or defective products.
  - o **Return Costs:** Determine who is responsible for return shipping costs.
- **Business Experience and Reputation:**
  - o **Years in Business:** Look for suppliers with a proven track record and experience in dropshipping.
  - o **Online Presence:** Check for a professional website and social media presence.
- **Production Capabilities and Inventory:**

- o **Production Capacity:** Inquire about the supplier's production capacity to ensure they can handle your order volume.
- o **Inventory Management:** Understand how the supplier manages inventory to avoid stockouts and delays.
- **Customer Service:**
  - o **Support Channels:** Inquire about the supplier's customer support channels, such as email, phone, or live chat.
  - o **Response Times:** Assess their responsiveness to customer inquiries and complaints.
- **Legal and Ethical Considerations:**
  - o **Business Legitimacy:** Verify the supplier's business legitimacy and registration.
  - o **Ethical Practices:** Choose suppliers who adhere to ethical business practices and responsible sourcing.

Expanding on Key Concepts

1. Building Strong Supplier Relationships

Developing strong relationships with your suppliers is crucial for long-term success in dropshipping. Here are some tips:

- **Communicate Clearly and Professionally:** Maintain clear and professional communication with your suppliers. Be respectful and responsive to their inquiries.
- **Provide Accurate Information:** Ensure you provide accurate order information and customer details to avoid delays or errors.
- **Pay on Time:** Pay your invoices promptly to maintain a good standing with your suppliers.
- **Address Issues Promptly:** If any issues arise, address them promptly and professionally. Work collaboratively with your supplier to find solutions.
- **Offer Constructive Feedback:** Provide constructive feedback to your suppliers about their products, services, or processes.

- **Build Trust and Mutual Respect:** Treat your suppliers as partners and build a relationship based on trust and mutual respect.
- **Negotiate Favorable Terms:** As your business grows, negotiate favorable terms with your suppliers, such as volume discounts or faster shipping options.

2. Understanding Supplier Pricing Models

Suppliers use different pricing models, and it's important to understand how they work to calculate your profit margins accurately. Here are some common pricing models:

- **Wholesale Pricing:** Suppliers offer products at a discounted wholesale price, which is lower than the retail price.
- **Volume Discounts:** Suppliers may offer discounts for larger orders, allowing you to increase your profit margins.
- **Tiered Pricing:** Suppliers may have different pricing tiers based on order volume or customer status.
- **Membership Fees:** Some suppliers may require a membership fee to access their products or services.
- **Dropshipping Fees:** Some suppliers may charge a per-order dropshipping fee to cover their fulfillment costs.

When evaluating suppliers, compare their pricing models and factor in any additional fees to determine the true cost of goods.

3. Managing Multiple Suppliers

Working with multiple suppliers can offer benefits like a wider product selection and reduced risk of stockouts. However, it also adds complexity to your operations. Here are some tips for managing multiple suppliers:

- **Centralize Communication:** Use a central platform or tool to manage communication with all your suppliers.
- **Track Supplier Performance:** Monitor each supplier's performance in terms of product quality, shipping times, and customer service.

- **Diversify Your Product Sourcing:** Avoid relying too heavily on a single supplier. Spread your product sourcing across multiple suppliers to mitigate risks.
- **Maintain Consistent Branding:** Ensure consistent branding across all your products, regardless of the supplier.
- **Streamline Order Fulfillment:** Use tools or apps to automate order fulfillment and track shipments from different suppliers.

4. Avoiding Common Supplier Issues

Here are some common supplier issues to watch out for and how to avoid them:

- **Inconsistent Product Quality:** Order samples and thoroughly vet suppliers to ensure consistent product quality.
- **Slow Shipping Times:** Clarify shipping times and options upfront and choose suppliers with reliable shipping methods.
- **Poor Communication:** Establish clear communication channels and expectations with your suppliers.
- **Inventory Issues:** Inquire about the supplier's inventory management practices to avoid stockouts and delays.
- **Hidden Fees:** Clarify all fees and costs associated with working with the supplier, including dropshipping fees, membership fees, or minimum order requirements.
- **Unreliable Order Fulfillment:** Choose suppliers with a proven track record of fulfilling orders accurately and on time.
- **Lack of Customer Support:** Ensure the supplier offers adequate customer support to address any issues that may arise.

5. Legal and Ethical Considerations when Sourcing Suppliers

When sourcing suppliers, it's important to consider legal and ethical aspects:

- **Product Safety and Compliance:** Ensure the supplier's products meet all relevant safety standards and regulations.

- **Intellectual Property Rights:** Verify that the supplier has the right to sell the products they offer and that they are not counterfeit or infringing on intellectual property rights.
- **Ethical Sourcing and Labor Practices:** Choose suppliers who adhere to ethical sourcing practices and fair labor standards.
- **Environmental Sustainability:** Consider suppliers who prioritize environmental sustainability and minimize their environmental impact.

By considering these legal and ethical factors, you can build a responsible and sustainable dropshipping business.

In Conclusion

Sourcing reliable suppliers is essential for dropshipping success. Platforms like AliExpress, Spocket, and SaleHoo offer various options to find suppliers. Remember to thoroughly evaluate supplier reliability based on factors like product quality, shipping times, communication, and customer service. Building strong supplier relationships is crucial for long-term success. By following these guidelines and staying informed about best practices, you can establish a strong supplier network and provide a positive experience for your customers.

Chapter 7: Setting Up Your Shopify Store

Ready to build your online store? This chapter provides a step-by-step guide to creating your Shopify account and configuring essential store settings. We'll cover everything from choosing a plan to setting up payment gateways, ensuring a smooth and efficient setup process.

Creating Your Shopify Account

1. **Start Your Free Trial:** Visit the Shopify website and sign up for a free trial. This allows you to explore the platform and its features before committing to a paid plan.
2. **Choose a Plan:** Shopify offers various plans with different features and pricing. Consider your budget and business needs when selecting a plan.
3. **Enter Your Store Name:** Choose a unique and memorable name for your store. This will be part of your store's web address (e.g., yourstorename.myshopify.com).
4. **Provide Basic Information:** Fill in your personal and business information, including your name, address, and contact details.
5. **Customize Your Store's Currency:** Select the currency you want to use for your store. This should align with your target market.
6. **Complete the Setup:** Follow the on-screen instructions to complete the initial setup process. This may involve answering questions about your business and goals.

Configuring Essential Store Settings

Once you've created your account, it's time to configure essential store settings.

1. General Settings:

- **Store Details:** Review and update your store name, contact information, and address.
- **Store Currency:** Confirm your store currency and ensure it's correct.
- **Standards and Formats:** Set your preferred standards for time zones, units of measurement, and date formats.

2. Payment Providers:

- **Select a Payment Gateway:** Choose a payment gateway that allows you to accept payments from customers. Popular options include Shopify Payments, PayPal, Stripe, and Authorize.net.
- **Configure Payment Settings:** Enter your payment gateway credentials and configure any necessary settings.

3. Checkout Settings:

- **Customer Accounts:** Decide whether to require customers to create accounts or allow guest checkout.
- **Customer Contact:** Choose how you want to collect customer contact information (email, phone number).
- **Order Processing:** Configure order processing settings, such as order confirmation emails and abandoned cart recovery.

4. Shipping Settings:

- **Shipping Zones:** Define shipping zones based on customer location.
- **Shipping Rates:** Set shipping rates for each zone, considering factors like product weight, dimensions, and shipping method.
- **Shipping Carriers:** Connect with shipping carriers like USPS, FedEx, or UPS to offer various shipping options.

5. Taxes:

- **Tax Settings:** Configure tax settings based on your business location and nexus.
- **Tax Rates:** Set tax rates for different regions and products.

- **Tax Exemptions:** Apply tax exemptions for specific products or customer groups.

6. Notifications:

- **Email Notifications:** Customize email notifications for orders, shipments, and customer inquiries.
- **SMS Notifications:** Set up SMS notifications for order updates or marketing messages (if applicable).

7. Legal:

- **Refund Policy:** Create a clear and concise refund policy.
- **Privacy Policy:** Develop a privacy policy that outlines how you collect, use, and protect customer data.
- **Terms of Service:** Draft terms of service that govern the use of your website and services.

Expanding on Key Concepts

1. Choosing a Shopify Plan

Shopify offers various plans to suit different business needs and budgets:

- **Basic Shopify:** The most affordable plan, suitable for new businesses with basic needs.
- **Shopify:** The standard plan, offering more features and lower transaction fees.
- **Advanced Shopify:** The premium plan, providing advanced features like advanced reporting and real-time carrier shipping rates.
- **Shopify Plus:** An enterprise-level solution for high-volume businesses with custom needs.

Consider factors like your sales volume, feature requirements, and budget when choosing a plan. You can always upgrade or downgrade your plan as your business grows.

2. Setting Up Payment Gateways

Choosing the right payment gateway is crucial for accepting payments securely and efficiently. Here are some popular options:

- **Shopify Payments:** Shopify's own payment gateway, offering seamless integration and competitive rates.
- **PayPal:** A widely recognized and trusted payment gateway with a large user base.
- **Stripe:** A popular payment gateway known for its developer-friendly API and security features.
- **Authorize.net:** A well-established payment gateway offering various payment options and fraud prevention tools.

When choosing a payment gateway, consider factors like transaction fees, supported currencies, security features, and customer preferences.

3. Configuring Shipping Settings

Setting up shipping correctly is essential for providing accurate shipping costs and delivery times to your customers. Here are some key considerations:

- **Shipping Zones:** Create shipping zones based on geographical regions or countries you ship to.
- **Shipping Rates:** Offer various shipping rates based on factors like product weight, dimensions, shipping destination, and shipping speed.
- **Real-time Carrier Shipping Rates:** Consider using real-time carrier shipping rates to provide accurate shipping costs at checkout.
- **Free Shipping:** Offer free shipping as an incentive to encourage customers to purchase.
- **Local Pickup:** If you offer local pickup, configure the settings and provide clear instructions for customers.

4. Managing Taxes Effectively

Collecting and remitting sales tax is a crucial aspect of running an online store. Here are some tips for managing taxes effectively:

- **Understand Nexus:** Determine where you have nexus and are required to collect sales tax.
- **Use Shopify's Tax Settings:** Configure Shopify's tax settings to automatically calculate and collect sales tax based on customer location.
- **Consider Tax Apps:** Explore third-party tax apps that can automate tax calculations and filing.
- **Keep Accurate Records:** Maintain detailed records of all sales transactions and tax collected.
- **Consult with a Tax Professional:** If you have complex tax requirements, consult with a tax professional for guidance.

5. Creating Essential Legal Pages

Having clear and comprehensive legal pages is important for protecting your business and building trust with your customers. Here are some essential pages to create:

- **Refund Policy:** Clearly outline your refund policy, including eligibility criteria, return process, and refund timeframe.
- **Privacy Policy:** Explain how you collect, use, and protect customer data. Be transparent about your data practices.
- **Terms of Service:** Define the terms and conditions governing the use of your website and services. Include provisions related to intellectual property, user conduct, and limitations of liability.

You can use Shopify's templates or consult with a legal professional to create these pages.

6. Optimizing Your Store for Mobile Devices

With the increasing use of mobile devices for online shopping, it's crucial to ensure your store is optimized for mobile. Here are some tips:

- **Choose a Responsive Theme:** Select a Shopify theme that is responsive and adapts to different screen sizes.
- **Optimize Images:** Use optimized images that load quickly on mobile devices.

- **Simplify Navigation:** Make your store easy to navigate on mobile devices with clear menus and buttons.
- **Test on Different Devices:** Test your store on various mobile devices to ensure it looks and functions correctly.

7. Adding Essential Apps

Shopify's app store offers a wide range of apps that can enhance your store's functionality and automate tasks. Here are some essential apps to consider:

- **Dropshipping Apps:** Integrate with dropshipping platforms like AliExpress, Spocket, or SaleHoo to streamline product sourcing and order fulfillment.
- **Marketing Apps:** Use marketing apps for email marketing, social media marketing, and search engine optimization.
- **Customer Service Apps:** Enhance customer service with apps for live chat, help desk ticketing, and customer reviews.
- **Analytics Apps:** Gain deeper insights into your store's performance with analytics apps that track key metrics.

In Conclusion

Setting up your Shopify store involves creating an account, choosing a plan, and configuring essential store settings. By following this step-by-step guide and paying attention to key details, you can create a functional and professional online store that's ready to welcome customers. Remember to optimize your store for mobile devices, add essential apps, and create clear legal pages to enhance your store's performance and build trust with your audience.

Chapter 8: Designing Your Store

Your online store is your digital storefront. It's the first impression customers get of your brand and products. This chapter guides you through designing an appealing and user-friendly Shopify store. We'll cover choosing a theme, customizing your store's appearance, and optimizing for a positive user experience.

Choosing a Theme

Your Shopify theme provides the basic framework and design for your store. Here's how to choose one that fits your needs:

- **Browse the Theme Store:** Shopify offers a vast collection of free and paid themes in its Theme Store. Explore different options and preview them to see how they look and function.
- **Consider Your Niche:** Choose a theme that aligns with your niche and target audience. A minimalist theme might suit a tech product store, while a vibrant theme might be better for a fashion boutique.
- **Prioritize Mobile Responsiveness:** Ensure the theme is mobile-responsive, adapting seamlessly to different screen sizes. Most Shopify themes are mobile-friendly, but it's crucial to double-check.
- **Look for Essential Features:** Consider features like product filtering, zoom functionality, and multiple product images. These can enhance the user experience.
- **Check for Customization Options:** Choose a theme that offers flexibility for customization. You'll want to personalize colors, fonts, and layout to match your brand.
- **Read Reviews and Ratings:** See what other users say about the theme. Look for themes with positive reviews and good support.

Customizing Your Store's Appearance

Once you've chosen a theme, it's time to customize it to match your brand and create a unique look.

- **Homepage:**
    - **Slider or Hero Image:** Use a high-quality image or slider to showcase your best products or promotions.
    - **Featured Products:** Highlight your most popular or newest products.
    - **About Us Section:** Introduce your brand and tell your story.
    - **Call to Action:** Encourage visitors to explore your store or sign up for your email list.
- **Product Pages:**
    - **High-Quality Images:** Use clear, professional product images from multiple angles.
    - **Detailed Descriptions:** Write compelling product descriptions that highlight key features and benefits.
    - **Customer Reviews:** Display customer reviews to build trust and social proof.
    - **Related Products:** Suggest related products to encourage further browsing and purchases.
- **Navigation:**
    - **Clear Menu Structure:** Organize your products into clear and logical categories.
    - **Search Bar:** Make it easy for customers to find specific products.
    - **Breadcrumbs:** Help customers understand their location within your store.
- **Branding:**
    - **Logo:** Prominently display your logo.
    - **Color Scheme:** Use a consistent color scheme that reflects your brand identity.
    - **Fonts:** Choose fonts that are easy to read and match your brand style.
- **Content Pages:**
    - **About Us:** Tell your brand story and connect with your audience.
    - **Contact Us:** Provide clear contact information and a contact form.
    - **FAQ:** Answer common customer questions.

o **Blog:** Share valuable content related to your niche.

Optimizing for User Experience

A positive user experience (UX) is crucial for attracting and retaining customers. Here's how to optimize your store for UX:

- **Site Speed:**
  - o **Optimize Images:** Compress images to reduce file size and improve loading speed.
  - o **Minimize Apps:** Only use essential apps to avoid slowing down your store.
  - o **Use a Content Delivery Network (CDN):** A CDN can help deliver your store's content faster to users around the world.
- **Navigation:**
  - o **Clear and Intuitive Menu:** Make it easy for customers to find what they're looking for.
  - o **Search Functionality:** Provide a robust search bar with filters and suggestions.
  - o **Mobile-Friendly Navigation:** Ensure your navigation works smoothly on mobile devices.
- **Product Pages:**
  - o **High-Quality Images:** Use large, zoomable product images.
  - o **Detailed Descriptions:** Provide comprehensive product information, including features, benefits, and specifications.
  - o **Customer Reviews:** Display customer reviews to build trust and social proof.
  - o **Clear Call to Action:** Make it easy for customers to add products to their cart and proceed to checkout.
- **Checkout Process:**
  - o **Guest Checkout:** Offer a guest checkout option to avoid forcing customers to create accounts.
  - o **Multiple Payment Options:** Provide various payment options to cater to different customer preferences.
  - o **Clear Progress Indicators:** Show customers their progress through the checkout process.

- o **Secure Checkout:** Ensure your checkout process is secure and protects customer data.
- **Mobile Optimization:**
  - o **Responsive Design:** Use a mobile-responsive theme that adapts to different screen sizes.
  - o **Touch-Friendly Elements:** Ensure buttons and links are large enough to tap on mobile devices.
  - o **Fast Loading Speed:** Optimize your store for fast loading speed on mobile devices.
- **Accessibility:**
  - o **Alt Text for Images:** Add alt text to images for visually impaired users.
  - o **Keyboard Navigation:** Ensure your store can be navigated using a keyboard.
  - o **Color Contrast:** Use sufficient color contrast for readability.

Expanding on Key Concepts

1. Understanding User Experience (UX)

User experience (UX) encompasses all aspects of a user's interaction with a product or service. In the context of an online store, UX refers to how easy and enjoyable it is for customers to browse, find products, and make purchases. A positive UX can lead to increased customer satisfaction, higher conversion rates, and repeat business.

2. Elements of Good UX Design

Several key elements contribute to a good UX design:

- **Usability:** The website should be easy to use and navigate.
- **Accessibility:** The website should be accessible to all users, including those with disabilities.
- **Findability:** Customers should be able to find what they're looking for quickly and easily.
- **Desirability:** The website should be visually appealing and engaging.
- **Credibility:** The website should build trust and credibility with users.

- **Value:** The website should provide value to users, whether through information, products, or services.

3. Tools for UX Optimization

Several tools can help you optimize your store's UX:

- **Google Analytics:** Track user behavior on your website, including page views, bounce rate, and conversion rate.
- **Hotjar:** Use heatmaps and recordings to see how users interact with your website.
- **UserTesting:** Get feedback from real users on their experience with your website.
- **Google PageSpeed Insights:** Analyze your website's loading speed and identify areas for improvement.
- **GTmetrix:** Another tool for analyzing website speed and performance.

4. A/B Testing for UX Improvement

A/B testing involves comparing two versions of a webpage or element to see which performs better. You can use A/B testing to test different design elements, calls to action, or layouts to see what resonates best with your audience.

5. The Importance of Mobile Optimization

With the majority of online traffic now coming from mobile devices, optimizing your store for mobile is essential. Here are some additional tips:

- **Use a Mobile-First Indexing:** Google uses mobile-first indexing, meaning it primarily uses the mobile version of your website for indexing and ranking.
- **Optimize for Mobile Speed:** Mobile users expect fast loading times. Compress images, minimize code, and use a CDN to improve mobile speed.
- **Design for Touch:** Ensure buttons and links are large enough to tap on mobile devices.

- **Simplify Forms:** Make forms short and easy to fill out on mobile devices.
- **Use a Sticky Header:** Keep your main navigation menu visible as users scroll on mobile devices.

6. Accessibility Considerations

Making your store accessible to all users, including those with disabilities, is not only ethically important but also good for business. Here are some accessibility tips:

- **Use Sufficient Color Contrast:** Ensure there is enough contrast between text and background colors for readability.
- **Provide Text Alternatives for Images:** Add alt text to images for users who use screen readers.
- **Use Clear and Simple Language:** Avoid jargon and complex terminology.
- **Structure Content Logically:** Use headings, subheadings, and lists to organize content.
- **Provide Keyboard Navigation:** Ensure users can navigate your store using a keyboard.
- **Use ARIA Attributes:** Use ARIA attributes to provide additional context and information for assistive technologies.

In Conclusion

Designing an appealing and user-friendly Shopify store involves choosing the right theme, customizing its appearance, and optimizing for a positive user experience. By following these guidelines and paying attention to key details, you can create an online store that attracts customers, showcases your products effectively, and encourages conversions. Remember to prioritize mobile optimization, accessibility, and continuous improvement to provide the best possible experience for your audience.

Chapter 9: Search Engine Optimization (SEO)

Want free, consistent traffic to your dropshipping store? Search Engine Optimization (SEO) is your answer. This chapter dives into SEO basics, focusing on keyword research, on-page optimization, and link building. We'll equip you with the knowledge to improve your store's visibility in search results and attract organic traffic.

What is SEO?

SEO is the practice of optimizing your website to rank higher in search engine results pages (SERPs). When someone searches for products you sell, you want your store to appear on the first page of results, ideally near the top. Higher rankings mean more visibility, clicks, and potential customers.

Why SEO Matters for Dropshipping

- **Targeted Traffic:** SEO brings in visitors actively looking for what you offer.
- **Cost-Effectiveness:** Organic traffic from SEO is free, unlike paid advertising.
- **Brand Credibility:** High search rankings boost your store's credibility and trustworthiness.
- **Long-Term Growth:** SEO builds sustainable traffic over time, unlike short-term boosts from ads.
- **Competitive Edge:** Strong SEO can give you an edge in a competitive dropshipping market.

Keyword Research

Keywords are the words and phrases people use in search engines. Effective keyword research helps you understand what your target audience is searching for.

- **Brainstorming:** Start by brainstorming a list of relevant keywords related to your products and niche.
- **Keyword Research Tools:** Use tools like Google Keyword Planner, Ahrefs, or SEMrush to:
    - **Discover New Keywords:** Find related keywords you might not have thought of.
    - **Analyze Search Volume:** See how many people search for specific keywords.
    - **Assess Competition:** Gauge how difficult it is to rank for certain keywords.
- **Long-Tail Keywords:** Focus on long-tail keywords (longer, more specific phrases) as they often have less competition. For example, instead of "women's shoes," target "comfortable women's running shoes for wide feet."
- **Keyword Mapping:** Organize your keywords by category and relevance to different pages on your site.

On-Page Optimization

On-page optimization refers to optimizing elements on your website to improve search rankings.

- **Title Tags:** Write unique, descriptive title tags for each page that include relevant keywords.
- **Meta Descriptions:** Craft compelling meta descriptions (short summaries that appear in search results) to encourage clicks.
- **Header Tags (H1, H2, etc.):** Use header tags to structure your content and incorporate keywords naturally.
- **Product Descriptions:** Write detailed, informative product descriptions with relevant keywords.
- **Image Optimization:** Use descriptive file names for images and add alt text (alternative text that describes the image).
- **URL Structure:** Use short, descriptive URLs that include relevant keywords.
- **Internal Linking:** Link to other relevant pages within your store to improve site navigation and user experience.
- **Mobile Optimization:** Ensure your website is mobile-friendly. Google prioritizes mobile-first indexing.

- **Page Speed:** Optimize your website's loading speed. Faster sites rank better and provide a better user experience.

Link Building

Link building involves getting other websites to link to your store. Search engines see these links as votes of confidence, boosting your site's authority and rankings.

- **Content Marketing:** Create high-quality, informative content (blog posts, guides, infographics) that others will want to link to.
- **Guest Blogging:** Write guest posts for other websites in your niche, including a link back to your store.
- **Outreach:** Reach out to relevant websites and blogs, asking them to link to your content or products.
- **Social Media:** Promote your content on social media to increase visibility and potential for links.
- **Directory Submissions:** Submit your store to relevant online directories.
- **Product Reviews:** Encourage customers to leave reviews on your products or on external review sites.
- **Partnerships:** Collaborate with other businesses or influencers in your niche for link exchange opportunities.

Expanding on Key Concepts

1. Understanding Search Engine Algorithms

Search engines use complex algorithms to determine the ranking of websites in search results. These algorithms consider hundreds of factors, including:

- **Relevance:** How relevant your website's content is to the search query.
- **Authority:** How trustworthy and authoritative your website is, based on factors like backlinks and domain age.
- **User Experience:** How user-friendly your website is, including factors like page speed, mobile optimization, and navigation.

- **Content Quality:** How informative, engaging, and well-written your content is.
- **Technical SEO:** Technical aspects of your website, such as site structure, crawlability, and security.

By understanding these factors, you can optimize your store to align with search engine algorithms and improve your rankings.

2. Types of SEO

SEO can be broadly categorized into:

- **On-Page SEO:** Optimizing elements on your website, as discussed earlier.
- **Off-Page SEO:** Building links and improving your website's authority through external factors.
- **Technical SEO:** Addressing technical aspects of your website to improve crawlability and indexability.

3. Tools for SEO

Several tools can help you with various aspects of SEO:

- **Google Search Console:** Provides insights into how Google sees your website, including indexing issues and search performance.
- **Google Analytics:** Tracks website traffic and user behavior, providing valuable data for SEO analysis.
- **Ahrefs and SEMrush:** Offer comprehensive SEO tools for keyword research, competitor analysis, backlink tracking, and more.
- **Moz:** Provides SEO tools and resources, including keyword research, rank tracking, and site audits.
- **Yoast SEO:** A popular plugin for WordPress that helps with on-page optimization.

4. Content Marketing for SEO

Creating high-quality content is a cornerstone of effective SEO. Here are some tips for content marketing:

- **Target Relevant Keywords:** Conduct keyword research to identify relevant keywords to target in your content.
- **Create Informative and Engaging Content:** Write content that provides value to your audience and answers their questions.
- **Use Different Content Formats:** Vary your content formats, including blog posts, articles, videos, infographics, and guides.
- **Promote Your Content:** Share your content on social media, email newsletters, and other channels.
- **Build Internal Links:** Link to other relevant content on your website to improve user experience and SEO.

5. Effective Link Building Strategies

Building high-quality backlinks is crucial for improving your website's authority and rankings. Here are some effective strategies:

- **Create Linkable Content:** Produce high-quality, informative content that others will want to link to.
- **Guest Blogging:** Write guest posts for other websites in your niche, including a link back to your store.
- **Broken Link Building:** Find broken links on other websites and offer your content as a replacement.
- **Resource Link Building:** Create a resource page on your website with valuable information and promote it to other websites.
- **Social Media Promotion:** Share your content on social media to increase visibility and attract links.
- **Directory Submissions:** Submit your website to relevant online directories.
- **Industry Forums and Communities:** Participate in industry forums and communities and include a link to your website in your profile.

6. Avoiding Black Hat SEO Tactics

Black hat SEO refers to unethical practices that try to manipulate search engine rankings. These tactics can lead to penalties and harm your website's reputation. Avoid practices like:

- **Keyword Stuffing:** Overusing keywords in your content.
- **Cloaking:** Showing different content to search engines than to users.
- **Link Farms:** Creating networks of websites solely for the purpose of link building.
- **Hidden Text:** Hiding text on your website to manipulate keyword rankings.
- **Buying Links:** Purchasing links from low-quality or irrelevant websites.

Focus on ethical, white hat SEO practices that provide value to your audience and align with search engine guidelines.

In Conclusion

SEO is a powerful tool for driving organic traffic to your dropshipping store. By conducting thorough keyword research, optimizing your website's content and structure, and building high-quality backlinks, you can improve your search rankings and attract more potential customers. Remember to focus on ethical SEO practices, create valuable content, and prioritize user experience to achieve long-term success.

Chapter 10: Paid Advertising

Want to reach your target audience quickly and directly? Paid advertising can be a powerful tool for dropshippers. This chapter focuses on two major platforms: Facebook Ads and Google Ads. We'll explore how to create effective campaigns, target the right audience, and maximize your return on investment.

Why Use Paid Advertising?

- **Fast Results:** Unlike SEO, which takes time, paid ads can drive traffic to your store immediately.
- **Precise Targeting:** Reach specific demographics, interests, and behaviors.
- **Increased Brand Awareness:** Boost your brand's visibility and reach a wider audience.
- **Measurable Results:** Track your ad performance and measure your return on investment (ROI).
- **Flexibility:** Adjust your campaigns and budgets as needed based on performance.

Facebook Ads

Facebook Ads allow you to reach a massive audience within the Facebook ecosystem, including Instagram.

- **Campaign Objectives:** Start by defining your campaign objective:
  - **Brand Awareness:** Increase brand visibility and reach.
  - **Traffic:** Drive traffic to your website.
  - **Conversions:** Encourage specific actions, like purchases or sign-ups.
- **Targeting Options:** Facebook offers detailed targeting options:

- o **Demographics:** Age, gender, location, language, education, etc.
- o **Interests:** Pages they like, topics they follow, etc.
- o **Behaviors:** Purchase history, device usage, etc.
- o **Custom Audiences:** Target people who have interacted with your website or Facebook page.
- o **Lookalike Audiences:** Reach people similar to your existing customers.
- **Ad Formats:** Choose the right ad format for your objective:
  - o **Image Ads:** Simple and effective for showcasing products.
  - o **Video Ads:** Engage viewers with dynamic content.
  - o **Carousel Ads:** Display multiple products or features.
  - o **Collection Ads:** Showcase a collection of products in a visually appealing way.
- **Ad Creative:** Create compelling ad copy and visuals that grab attention and encourage clicks.
- **Budget and Bidding:** Set a daily or lifetime budget and choose a bidding strategy (automatic or manual).
- **Tracking and Optimization:** Monitor your ad performance and make adjustments to improve results.

Google Ads

Google Ads display your ads on Google's search results pages and other Google properties.

- **Keyword Targeting:** Choose relevant keywords that potential customers are likely to search for.
- **Match Types:** Select match types to control how closely your keywords match search queries:
  - o **Broad Match:** Reaches the widest audience but may include irrelevant searches.
  - o **Phrase Match:** Matches searches that include your keyword phrase in the same order.
  - o **Exact Match:** Matches only searches that exactly match your keyword.
- **Ad Formats:** Google Ads offer various ad formats:
  - o **Text Ads:** Simple text-based ads that appear on search results pages.

- o **Shopping Ads:** Display product images and prices directly in search results.
- o **Display Ads:** Visual ads that appear on websites across the Google Display Network.
- o **Video Ads:** Run video ads on YouTube and other Google properties.
- **Ad Copy:** Write clear and concise ad copy that highlights your unique selling propositions and includes a strong call to action.
- **Landing Pages:** Create dedicated landing pages that align with your ad copy and offer a relevant user experience.
- **Budget and Bidding:** Set a daily or monthly budget and choose a bidding strategy (automatic or manual).
- **Tracking and Optimization:** Use Google Ads tools to track your ad performance and make data-driven optimizations.

Expanding on Key Concepts

1. Developing a Paid Advertising Strategy

Before launching any paid advertising campaigns, it's essential to develop a clear strategy:

- **Define Your Goals:** What do you want to achieve with your ads? (e.g., increase brand awareness, drive traffic, generate leads, boost sales)
- **Identify Your Target Audience:** Who are you trying to reach with your ads? (e.g., demographics, interests, behaviors)
- **Choose the Right Platforms:** Which platforms are best suited for reaching your target audience? (e.g., Facebook, Instagram, Google Search, YouTube)
- **Set a Budget:** How much are you willing to spend on paid advertising?
- **Develop Compelling Ad Creative:** Create ad copy and visuals that grab attention and encourage clicks.
- **Track Your Results:** Monitor your ad performance and make adjustments to improve results.

2. Creating Effective Facebook Ads

Here are some tips for creating effective Facebook Ads:

- **Use High-Quality Images or Videos:** Visuals are crucial for grabbing attention on Facebook. Use high-quality images or videos that are relevant to your products or brand.
- **Write Engaging Ad Copy:** Keep your ad copy concise and attention-grabbing. Highlight your unique selling propositions and include a clear call to action.
- **Target the Right Audience:** Use Facebook's detailed targeting options to reach the most relevant audience for your products.
- **Test Different Ad Formats:** Experiment with different ad formats to see what works best for your objectives.
- **Monitor and Optimize Your Campaigns:** Track your ad performance and make adjustments to improve results.

3. Optimizing Google Ads Campaigns

Here are some strategies for optimizing your Google Ads campaigns:

- **Conduct Thorough Keyword Research:** Choose relevant keywords that potential customers are likely to search for.
- **Use Negative Keywords:** Exclude irrelevant keywords to improve your targeting and reduce wasted ad spend.
- **Write Compelling Ad Copy:** Highlight your unique selling propositions and include a strong call to action.
- **Create Dedicated Landing Pages:** Ensure your landing pages align with your ad copy and offer a relevant user experience.
- **Use Ad Extensions:** Add ad extensions to provide more information and encourage clicks.
- **Monitor and Adjust Bids:** Regularly monitor your bids and adjust them based on performance.
- **Use A/B Testing:** Test different ad variations to see what performs best.

4. Tracking and Measuring Results

Tracking and measuring your paid advertising results is crucial for understanding what's working and optimizing your campaigns. Here are some key metrics to track:

- **Impressions:** The number of times your ad was shown.
- **Clicks:** The number of times your ad was clicked.
- **Click-Through Rate (CTR):** The percentage of people who clicked on your ad after seeing it.
- **Conversion Rate:** The percentage of people who completed a desired action (e.g., purchase, sign-up) after clicking on your ad.
- **Cost per Click (CPC):** The average cost you pay for each click on your ad.
- **Cost per Conversion:** The average cost you pay for each conversion.
- **Return on Ad Spend (ROAS):** The revenue generated for every dollar spent on advertising.

Use the tracking tools provided by Facebook Ads and Google Ads to monitor these metrics and make data-driven decisions.

5. Retargeting Campaigns

Retargeting allows you to show ads to people who have previously interacted with your website or Facebook page. This can be an effective way to re-engage potential customers and encourage them to complete a purchase.

6. Remarketing with Google Ads

Remarketing with Google Ads allows you to show ads to people who have previously visited your website. You can create different audience lists based on user behavior, such as visitors who abandoned their shopping cart or viewed specific product pages.

7. Dynamic Remarketing

Dynamic remarketing takes remarketing a step further by showing ads that feature the specific products or services that users previously viewed on your website. This can be a highly effective way to re-engage potential customers and encourage them to return to your store.

In Conclusion

Paid advertising can be a valuable tool for dropshippers to reach their target audience, increase brand awareness, and drive sales. By understanding the different platforms, ad formats, and targeting options, you can create effective campaigns that generate a positive return on investment. Remember to track your results, make data-driven optimizations, and continuously refine your strategies to maximize your success with paid advertising.

Chapter 11: Social Media Marketing

Social media isn't just for connecting with friends and family. It's a powerful tool for dropshippers to reach potential customers and build a brand. This chapter focuses on two popular platforms: Instagram and TikTok. We'll explore how to leverage these platforms to promote your store, engage your audience, and drive sales.

Why Social Media Matters for Dropshipping

- **Massive Reach:** Billions of people use social media platforms, offering a vast potential audience.
- **Targeted Engagement:** Connect with specific demographics, interests, and behaviors.
- **Brand Building:** Create a strong brand identity and foster customer loyalty.
- **Visual Storytelling:** Showcase your products and brand story through compelling visuals.
- **Direct Connection:** Engage with customers directly, answer questions, and build relationships.
- **Traffic Generation:** Drive traffic to your Shopify store through social media links and calls to action.

Instagram Marketing

Instagram is a visual-centric platform perfect for showcasing products and lifestyle.

- **Create a Business Profile:** Set up an Instagram Business account to access analytics and advertising tools.
- **Content Strategy:** Plan your content to align with your brand and target audience.
  - **High-Quality Images and Videos:** Use visually appealing content that showcases your products in action.
  - **Stories:** Share behind-the-scenes content, product updates, and limited-time offers.

- o **Reels:** Create short, engaging videos to capture attention and entertain your audience.
- o **Livestreams:** Connect with your audience in real-time, answer questions, and showcase products.
- **Hashtags:** Use relevant hashtags to increase your content's visibility. Research popular hashtags in your niche.
- **Engagement:** Interact with your audience by responding to comments, messages, and mentions.
- **Influencer Marketing:** Collaborate with influencers in your niche to reach a wider audience.
- **Instagram Shopping:** Set up Instagram Shopping to allow users to purchase products directly within the app.
- **Paid Advertising:** Use Instagram Ads to reach a broader audience and promote specific products or offers.

TikTok Marketing

TikTok is a short-form video platform known for its viral potential and creative content.

- **Understand the Algorithm:** TikTok's algorithm prioritizes engaging content that keeps users watching.
- **Content Creation:**
  - o **Trend-Driven Content:** Create videos that align with current trends and challenges.
  - o **Product Demonstrations:** Showcase your products in creative and engaging ways.
  - o **Behind-the-Scenes:** Give viewers a glimpse into your business and brand personality.
  - o **User-Generated Content:** Encourage users to create content featuring your products.
- **Music and Sound Effects:** Use trending music and sound effects to enhance your videos.
- **Hashtags:** Use relevant hashtags to increase your video's visibility.
- **Engagement:** Interact with other users by commenting on their videos and participating in challenges.
- **Influencer Marketing:** Partner with TikTok creators to reach a wider audience.

- **TikTok Ads:** Utilize TikTok Ads to promote your videos and reach a targeted audience.

Expanding on Key Concepts

1. Developing a Social Media Strategy

Before diving into social media marketing, create a clear strategy:

- **Define Your Goals:** What do you want to achieve with social media? (e.g., brand awareness, traffic, sales, engagement)
- **Identify Your Target Audience:** Who are you trying to reach on social media? (e.g., demographics, interests, behaviors)
- **Choose the Right Platforms:** Which platforms are best suited for your target audience and goals?
- **Content Calendar:** Plan your content in advance to ensure consistency and variety.
- **Brand Guidelines:** Establish brand guidelines for your social media presence, including tone of voice, visual style, and content themes.
- **Analyze and Adjust:** Track your social media performance and make adjustments to your strategy as needed.

2. Creating Engaging Social Media Content

Here are some tips for creating engaging social media content:

- **Know Your Audience:** Understand your target audience's interests and preferences.
- **Use High-Quality Visuals:** Visuals are crucial for grabbing attention on social media. Use high-quality images and videos.
- **Tell a Story:** Use storytelling to connect with your audience and make your content more memorable.
- **Use Humor and Emotion:** Incorporate humor or emotion to make your content more relatable and shareable.
- **Ask Questions:** Encourage engagement by asking questions and prompting responses from your audience.

- **Run Contests and Giveaways:** Generate excitement and encourage participation with contests and giveaways.
- **Stay Consistent:** Post regularly to keep your audience engaged and coming back for more.

3. Building a Community on Social Media

Social media is about more than just broadcasting your message. It's about building a community around your brand. Here's how:

- **Respond to Comments and Messages:** Engage with your audience by responding to comments and messages promptly.
- **Ask for Feedback:** Encourage your audience to share their thoughts and opinions.
- **Create a Sense of Belonging:** Make your followers feel like they're part of a community by fostering a welcoming and inclusive environment.
- **Run Social Media Groups:** Create Facebook groups or other online communities where your audience can connect with each other and your brand.

4. Social Listening and Monitoring

Social listening involves monitoring social media conversations related to your brand, industry, or competitors. This can help you:

- **Identify Customer Sentiment:** Understand how people feel about your brand and products.
- **Discover Trends and Opportunities:** Stay informed about industry trends and identify potential opportunities.
- **Manage Your Reputation:** Address any negative feedback or concerns promptly.
- **Find Influencers:** Identify influencers who are talking about your industry or niche.

5. Using Social Media Analytics

Most social media platforms offer analytics tools that provide insights into your performance. Use these tools to:

- **Track Your Progress:** Monitor your follower growth, engagement rate, and reach.
- **Identify Top Performing Content:** See which types of content resonate most with your audience.
- **Measure Campaign Effectiveness:** Track the results of your social media campaigns and measure their ROI.
- **Understand Your Audience:** Gain insights into your audience's demographics, interests, and behaviors.

6. Social Media Advertising

Social media advertising allows you to reach a wider audience and promote specific products or offers. Here are some tips:

- **Set Clear Objectives:** Define your advertising goals, whether it's brand awareness, traffic, or conversions.
- **Target the Right Audience:** Use the platform's targeting options to reach the most relevant audience for your ads.
- **Create Compelling Ad Creative:** Develop ad copy and visuals that grab attention and encourage clicks.
- **Test Different Ad Formats:** Experiment with different ad formats to see what works best for your objectives.
- **Monitor and Optimize Your Campaigns:** Track your ad performance and make adjustments to improve results.

7. Influencer Marketing

Influencer marketing involves collaborating with influencers in your niche to promote your products or brand. Here are some tips:

- **Choose the Right Influencers:** Select influencers who align with your brand and target audience.
- **Set Clear Goals:** Define your objectives for the collaboration.
- **Provide Creative Freedom:** Allow influencers to create content that feels authentic to their audience.
- **Track Your Results:** Measure the impact of the collaboration on your brand awareness, traffic, or sales.

In Conclusion

Social media marketing is a powerful tool for dropshippers to reach their target audience, build a brand, and drive sales. By leveraging platforms like Instagram and TikTok, creating engaging content, and building a community around your brand, you can effectively promote your store and achieve your business goals. Remember to stay consistent, track your results, and adapt your strategies to the ever-evolving social media landscape.

Chapter 12: Email Marketing

Email marketing remains a powerful tool for connecting with customers and driving sales. This chapter guides you through building an email list and creating effective email campaigns. We'll explore strategies for attracting subscribers, crafting compelling emails, and maximizing your email marketing ROI.

Why Email Marketing Matters for Dropshipping

- **Direct Communication:** Reach your audience directly in their inboxes.
- **Build Relationships:** Nurture relationships with customers and foster loyalty.
- **Drive Sales:** Promote products, announce sales, and recover abandoned carts.
- **Targeted Messaging:** Segment your audience and send personalized emails.
- **Measurable Results:** Track email opens, clicks, and conversions to measure effectiveness.
- **Cost-Effectiveness:** Email marketing can be a cost-effective way to reach your audience.

Building Your Email List

Growing your email list is the first step to successful email marketing.

- **Offer Incentives:** Provide valuable incentives to encourage sign-ups:
  - **Discounts:** Offer a discount code for first-time subscribers.
  - **Free Shipping:** Provide free shipping for subscribers.
  - **Exclusive Content:** Offer access to exclusive content, like ebooks or guides.

- o **Contests and Giveaways:** Host contests or giveaways with email sign-up as an entry requirement.
- **Website Sign-Up Forms:** Place prominent sign-up forms on your website:
  - o **Pop-up Forms:** Use pop-up forms to capture attention and encourage sign-ups.
  - o **Embedded Forms:** Integrate sign-up forms into your website's layout, such as in the footer or sidebar.
- **Landing Pages:** Create dedicated landing pages for email sign-ups, highlighting the benefits of subscribing.
- **Social Media Promotion:** Promote your email list on your social media channels.
- **Content Upgrades:** Offer bonus content within your blog posts or articles in exchange for email sign-ups.
- **Offline Sign-Ups:** Collect email addresses at events or in-store (if applicable).

Creating Effective Email Campaigns

Once you have an email list, it's time to create compelling campaigns.

- **Welcome Emails:** Send a welcome email to new subscribers, thanking them for joining and setting expectations.
- **Promotional Emails:** Promote your products, announce sales, and highlight special offers.
- **Informational Emails:** Share valuable content, like blog posts, product guides, or industry news.
- **Transactional Emails:** Send order confirmations, shipping updates, and other transactional messages.
- **Abandoned Cart Emails:** Recover lost sales by sending emails to customers who abandoned their shopping carts.
- **Personalized Emails:** Segment your audience and send personalized emails based on their interests or purchase history.
- **Automated Email Sequences:** Create automated email sequences to nurture leads and guide customers through the sales funnel.

Email Best Practices

Follow these best practices to maximize your email marketing effectiveness:

- **Compelling Subject Lines:** Write subject lines that grab attention and encourage opens.
- **Clear and Concise Content:** Keep your emails focused and easy to read. Use clear and concise language.
- **Strong Call to Action:** Include a clear call to action in every email, telling subscribers what you want them to do.
- **Mobile Optimization:** Ensure your emails are mobile-friendly and display correctly on different devices.
- **Segmentation:** Segment your audience to send more targeted and relevant emails.
- **Personalization:** Use personalization tokens to address subscribers by name and tailor content to their interests.
- **A/B Testing:** Test different email elements, like subject lines or calls to action, to see what performs best.
- **Analytics Tracking:** Track email opens, clicks, and conversions to measure your campaign's effectiveness.
- **Compliance:** Comply with email marketing regulations, like the CAN-SPAM Act.

Expanding on Key Concepts

1. Types of Email Campaigns

Here's a closer look at different types of email campaigns:

- **Welcome Series:** A series of emails that welcome new subscribers, introduce your brand, and set expectations.
- **Promotional Campaigns:** Focus on promoting specific products or offers.
- **Content Newsletters:** Share valuable content, like blog posts, articles, or videos.
- **Seasonal Campaigns:** Promote products or offers relevant to specific seasons or holidays.
- **Trigger-Based Campaigns:** Triggered by specific actions, like abandoned carts or birthdays.

- **Re-engagement Campaigns:** Target inactive subscribers to re-engage them with your brand.

2. Email Segmentation Strategies

Segmenting your email list allows you to send more targeted and relevant emails. Here are some segmentation strategies:

- **Demographics:** Segment by age, gender, location, or other demographic factors.
- **Purchase History:** Segment based on past purchases or product interests.
- **Engagement Level:** Segment based on email opens, clicks, or website activity.
- **Lifecycle Stage:** Segment based on where subscribers are in the customer journey (e.g., new subscriber, repeat customer).

3. Crafting Compelling Email Subject Lines

Your email subject line is the first thing subscribers see. It plays a crucial role in determining whether they open your email. Here are some tips:

- **Keep it Concise:** Aim for subject lines that are 60 characters or less.
- **Use Personalization:** Include the subscriber's name or other personal details.
- **Create Urgency:** Use words like "now" or "limited time" to create a sense of urgency.
- **Ask a Question:** Pose a question that piques the subscriber's curiosity.
- **Offer Value:** Clearly state the benefit of opening the email.
- **Avoid Spam Trigger Words:** Avoid using words like "free" or "guarantee" that can trigger spam filters.

4. Email Design and Formatting

The design and formatting of your emails can impact their readability and effectiveness. Here are some tips:

- **Use a Clean and Simple Layout:** Avoid clutter and use a clear visual hierarchy.
- **Choose Easy-to-Read Fonts:** Use fonts that are easy to read on different devices.
- **Use Whitespace Effectively:** Break up text with whitespace to improve readability.
- **Include Visuals:** Use images or videos to enhance your email's visual appeal.
- **Optimize for Mobile:** Ensure your emails display correctly on different screen sizes.

5. Email Marketing Automation

Email marketing automation allows you to send emails automatically based on specific triggers or schedules. This can save you time and improve your campaign's efficiency. Here are some automation ideas:

- **Welcome Email Series:** Automatically send a series of welcome emails to new subscribers.
- **Abandoned Cart Emails:** Trigger emails to customers who abandon their shopping carts.
- **Birthday Emails:** Send personalized birthday emails to subscribers.
- **Post-Purchase Follow-Up:** Send follow-up emails after a purchase to thank customers and offer related products.

6. Email Marketing Tools

Several email marketing tools can help you manage your email list, create campaigns, and track your results. Here are some popular options:

- **Klaviyo:** A powerful email marketing platform with advanced segmentation and automation features.
- **Mailchimp:** A popular email marketing service with a user-friendly interface and various pricing plans.
- **Omnisend:** An omnichannel marketing platform that integrates email, SMS, and push notifications.

- **ActiveCampaign:** An email marketing and automation platform with advanced features for lead nurturing and sales automation.

7. Measuring Email Marketing ROI

Tracking your email marketing results is crucial for understanding what's working and optimizing your campaigns. Here are some key metrics to track:

- **Open Rate:** The percentage of subscribers who opened your email.
- **Click-Through Rate (CTR):** The percentage of subscribers who clicked on a link in your email.
- **Conversion Rate:** The percentage of subscribers who completed a desired action (e.g., purchase, sign-up) after clicking on a link in your email.
- **Revenue:** The total revenue generated from your email campaigns.
- **Return on Investment (ROI):** The revenue generated for every dollar spent on email marketing.

In Conclusion

Email marketing is a valuable tool for dropshippers to build relationships with customers, promote products, and drive sales. By building an email list, creating effective email campaigns, and following best practices, you can maximize your email marketing ROI and achieve your business goals. Remember to segment your audience, personalize your messages, and track your results to continuously improve your email marketing effectiveness.

Chapter 13: Content Marketing

Content marketing is about creating and sharing valuable content to attract and engage potential customers. It's not about directly pushing your products but about providing helpful information that builds trust and establishes your brand as an authority. This chapter explores how to use blog posts, articles, videos, and other content to draw in customers and grow your dropshipping business.

Why Content Marketing Matters for Dropshipping

- **Attract Organic Traffic:** High-quality content can rank well in search results, bringing in free, targeted traffic to your store.
- **Build Trust and Credibility:** Informative content positions you as an expert in your niche, increasing customer trust.
- **Engage Your Audience:** Engaging content keeps people interested in your brand and coming back for more.
- **Generate Leads:** Offer valuable content in exchange for email sign-ups, building your email list.
- **Support Social Media Efforts:** Share your content on social media to increase reach and engagement.
- **Drive Sales:** Content can indirectly lead to sales by educating customers and building brand awareness.

Types of Content

You can create various types of content to attract and engage your audience:

- **Blog Posts:** Share informative articles, how-to guides, product reviews, or behind-the-scenes insights.
- **Articles:** Publish in-depth articles on topics related to your niche.
- **Videos:** Create product demonstrations, tutorials, or explainer videos.

- **Infographics:** Present data and information visually in an engaging way.
- **Ebooks and Guides:** Offer in-depth guides or ebooks on topics relevant to your audience.
- **Case Studies:** Showcase success stories or customer testimonials.
- **Social Media Content:** Create engaging posts, stories, and reels for your social media channels.
- **Email Newsletters:** Share valuable content and updates with your email subscribers.

Creating High-Quality Content

Here are some tips for creating content that resonates with your audience:

- **Know Your Audience:** Understand your target audience's interests, needs, and pain points.
- **Keyword Research:** Use keyword research to identify topics people are searching for.
- **Provide Value:** Offer informative, helpful, or entertaining content that addresses your audience's needs.
- **Use Engaging Formats:** Vary your content formats to keep your audience interested.
- **Write Clearly and Concisely:** Use clear and concise language that's easy to understand.
- **Optimize for SEO:** Optimize your content for search engines by using relevant keywords and following SEO best practices.
- **Promote Your Content:** Share your content on social media, email, and other channels.

Content Distribution and Promotion

Creating great content is only half the battle. You also need to distribute and promote it effectively.

- **Social Media Sharing:** Share your content on your social media channels, tailoring your message to each platform.

- **Email Marketing:** Promote your content in your email newsletters and send dedicated email blasts for new content.
- **Content Syndication:** Republish your content on other websites or platforms to reach a wider audience.
- **Paid Promotion:** Use paid advertising to promote your content on social media or search engines.
- **Influencer Marketing:** Collaborate with influencers to share your content with their audience.
- **Community Engagement:** Share your content in relevant online communities and forums.

Expanding on Key Concepts

1. Developing a Content Marketing Strategy

Before creating content, develop a clear strategy:

- **Define Your Goals:** What do you want to achieve with your content? (e.g., increase brand awareness, generate leads, drive traffic)
- **Identify Your Target Audience:** Who are you trying to reach with your content? (e.g., demographics, interests, needs)
- **Content Audit:** If you have existing content, conduct an audit to assess its effectiveness and identify gaps.
- **Content Calendar:** Plan your content in advance to ensure consistency and variety.
- **Choose the Right Formats:** Select content formats that align with your audience's preferences and your goals.
- **Promote Your Content:** Develop a plan for distributing and promoting your content.
- **Measure Your Results:** Track your content's performance and make adjustments to your strategy as needed.

2. Content Ideation and Planning

Coming up with fresh content ideas can be challenging. Here are some tips:

- **Brainstorming:** Gather your team or brainstorm on your own to generate content ideas.
- **Keyword Research:** Use keyword research tools to identify popular search terms and topics.
- **Competitor Analysis:** Analyze your competitors' content to see what's working for them.
- **Customer Feedback:** Pay attention to customer feedback and questions to identify content needs.
- **Industry Trends:** Stay updated on industry trends and news to find relevant content ideas.
- **Content Curation:** Curate and share relevant content from other sources.

3. Content Optimization for SEO

Optimizing your content for search engines can help you attract more organic traffic. Here are some tips:

- **Keyword Research:** Use relevant keywords throughout your content, including in the title, headings, and body text.
- **On-Page Optimization:** Follow on-page optimization best practices, such as using descriptive title tags and meta descriptions.
- **Link Building:** Build internal and external links to your content to improve its authority.
- **Content Structure:** Use headings, subheadings, and bullet points to structure your content for readability.
- **Image Optimization:** Optimize your images by using descriptive file names and alt text.

4. Content Promotion Strategies

Promoting your content is essential for reaching a wider audience. Here are some strategies:

- **Social Media Sharing:** Share your content on all your social media channels, tailoring your message to each platform.
- **Email Marketing:** Promote your content in your email newsletters and send dedicated email blasts for new content.

- **Content Syndication:** Republish your content on other websites or platforms to reach a wider audience.
- **Paid Promotion:** Use paid advertising to promote your content on social media or search engines.
- **Influencer Marketing:** Collaborate with influencers to share your content with their audience.
- **Community Engagement:** Share your content in relevant online communities and forums.

5. Repurposing Content

Repurposing content involves taking existing content and transforming it into a different format. This can help you reach a wider audience and extend the life of your content. Here are some examples:

- **Turn a blog post into a video.**
- **Create an infographic from a data-heavy article.**
- **Compile a series of blog posts into an ebook.**
- **Share excerpts from your content on social media.**

6. Measuring Content Marketing Success

Tracking your content marketing results is crucial for understanding what's working and optimizing your strategy. Here are some key metrics to track:

- **Website Traffic:** Monitor the number of visitors your content attracts to your website.
- **Engagement:** Track metrics like time on page, bounce rate, and social shares.
- **Leads:** Measure the number of leads generated from your content (e.g., email sign-ups).
- **Sales:** Track the number of sales that can be attributed to your content.
- **Social Media Engagement:** Monitor likes, comments, and shares on your social media content.

In Conclusion

Content marketing is a powerful tool for dropshippers to attract and engage potential customers. By creating high-quality content, optimizing it for search engines, and promoting it effectively, you can build brand awareness, generate leads, and drive sales. Remember to develop a clear content marketing strategy, track your results, and adapt your approach as needed to achieve your business goals.

Part 4: Operations and Growth

Chapter 14: Order Fulfillment and Customer Service

Order fulfillment and customer service are the backbone of any successful dropshipping business. This chapter delves into the processes involved in managing orders, tracking shipments, and providing excellent customer support. We'll explore how to streamline your operations, exceed customer expectations, and build a loyal customer base.

Order Fulfillment Process

While you don't handle inventory directly in dropshipping, you're still responsible for ensuring orders are processed and delivered smoothly.

1. **Order Received:** When a customer places an order on your Shopify store, you receive a notification.
2. **Review Order Details:** Check the order details, including product information, customer address, and shipping method.
3. **Forward Order to Supplier:** Place the order with your supplier, providing all necessary customer and shipping information. Many dropshipping apps automate this step.
4. **Supplier Processes Order:** The supplier processes the order, packages the product, and ships it directly to the customer.
5. **Order Tracking:** Provide the customer with a tracking number so they can monitor their shipment's progress.
6. **Order Confirmation and Updates:** Keep the customer informed throughout the process with order confirmation emails and shipping updates.
7. **Delivery:** The product is delivered to the customer.
8. **Order Completion:** Mark the order as complete in your Shopify admin.

Streamlining Order Fulfillment

Here are some ways to streamline your order fulfillment process:

- **Dropshipping Apps:** Use dropshipping apps like DSers or Oberlo to automate order forwarding and tracking.
- **Centralized Order Management:** Use a central platform or dashboard to manage orders from all sales channels.
- **Supplier Communication:** Establish clear communication channels with your suppliers to ensure efficient order processing.
- **Order Tracking System:** Implement an order tracking system to monitor shipments and provide updates to customers.
- **Shipping Optimization:** Negotiate with suppliers for faster shipping options or consider using multiple suppliers for quicker delivery times.

Providing Excellent Customer Service

Customer service is crucial in dropshipping, as you are the main point of contact for customers.

- **Responsiveness:** Respond to customer inquiries promptly, ideally within 24 hours.
- **Helpful and Informative:** Provide accurate information and assist customers with their needs.
- **Professionalism:** Maintain a professional and courteous demeanor in all customer interactions.
- **Empathy:** Show empathy and understanding when customers experience issues.
- **Solutions-Oriented:** Focus on finding solutions to customer problems and resolving issues efficiently.
- **Personalization:** Address customers by name and personalize your responses whenever possible.
- **Follow-Up:** Follow up with customers to ensure their issues are resolved and they are satisfied.

Handling Customer Inquiries

Here are some common types of customer inquiries and how to handle them:

- **Order Status:** Provide customers with tracking information and updates on their order status.
- **Shipping Questions:** Answer questions about shipping methods, delivery times, and shipping costs.
- **Product Information:** Provide detailed product information and answer questions about product features or specifications.
- **Returns and Refunds:** Handle return and refund requests promptly and according to your store's policies.
- **Complaints:** Address customer complaints professionally and work towards finding solutions.
- **Technical Issues:** Assist customers with technical issues related to your website or products.

Customer Service Channels

Offer multiple channels for customers to reach you:

- **Email:** Provide a dedicated customer service email address.
- **Live Chat:** Offer live chat support for immediate assistance.
- **Social Media:** Respond to customer inquiries and messages on your social media channels.
- **Phone Support:** Consider offering phone support for complex issues or personalized assistance.
- **FAQ Page:** Create a comprehensive FAQ page to answer common customer questions.

Expanding on Key Concepts

1. The Importance of Customer Service in Dropshipping

Customer service plays a vital role in dropshipping success. Here's why:

- **Builds Trust and Loyalty:** Excellent customer service fosters trust and encourages repeat business.
- **Enhances Brand Reputation:** Positive customer experiences contribute to a positive brand image.

- **Reduces Returns and Refunds:** Proactive customer service can help prevent issues that lead to returns and refunds.
- **Increases Customer Lifetime Value:** Satisfied customers are more likely to make repeat purchases and become loyal customers.
- **Provides Valuable Feedback:** Customer interactions can provide valuable insights into your products, services, and customer needs.

2. Creating a Customer Service Policy

Develop a clear customer service policy that outlines your:

- **Response Times:** Specify how quickly customers can expect a response to their inquiries.
- **Return and Refund Policy:** Clearly define your return and refund procedures.
- **Shipping Policy:** Outline your shipping methods, delivery times, and shipping costs.
- **Privacy Policy:** Explain how you collect, use, and protect customer data.
- **Contact Information:** Provide various ways for customers to contact you.

3. Using Customer Service Tools

Several tools can help you manage customer service efficiently:

- **Help Desk Software:** Use help desk software to track customer inquiries, manage tickets, and provide support.
- **Live Chat Software:** Integrate live chat software into your website for immediate customer assistance.
- **Email Management Tools:** Use email management tools to organize and respond to customer emails efficiently.
- **Social Media Management Tools:** Use social media management tools to monitor and respond to customer inquiries on your social media channels.
- **Knowledge Base Software:** Create a knowledge base or FAQ section to provide self-service support.

4. Dealing with Difficult Customers

While most customers are pleasant to interact with, you may encounter difficult customers from time to time. Here are some tips for handling them:

- **Stay Calm and Professional:** Maintain a calm and professional demeanor, even if the customer is upset.
- **Listen Actively:** Listen carefully to the customer's concerns and try to understand their perspective.
- **Show Empathy:** Acknowledge the customer's feelings and show empathy for their situation.
- **Offer Solutions:** Focus on finding solutions to the customer's problem.
- **Set Boundaries:** If the customer becomes abusive or unreasonable, set boundaries and politely end the interaction.

5. Measuring Customer Service Performance

Tracking your customer service performance can help you identify areas for improvement. Here are some key metrics to track:

- **Response Time:** Measure how quickly you respond to customer inquiries.
- **Resolution Time:** Track how long it takes to resolve customer issues.
- **Customer Satisfaction:** Use surveys or feedback forms to measure customer satisfaction.
- **Return and Refund Rate:** Monitor your return and refund rate to identify potential issues.
- **Customer Churn Rate:** Track the rate at which customers stop doing business with you.

6. Proactive Customer Service

Proactive customer service involves anticipating customer needs and addressing potential issues before they arise. Here are some examples:

- **Order Confirmation and Updates:** Send timely order confirmations and shipping updates to keep customers informed.
- **Product Information and Guides:** Provide detailed product information and helpful guides to answer common questions.
- **Personalized Recommendations:** Offer personalized product recommendations based on customer interests or purchase history.
- **Proactive Outreach:** Reach out to customers who have had a positive experience to thank them and offer support.

In Conclusion

Order fulfillment and customer service are critical components of a successful dropshipping business. By streamlining your order fulfillment process, providing excellent customer support, and handling customer inquiries effectively, you can build trust, enhance your brand reputation, and foster customer loyalty. Remember to use the right tools, track your performance, and continuously improve your customer service to exceed customer expectations and drive business growth.

Chapter 15: Analyzing and Improving Performance

Data is your best friend in the world of ecommerce. This chapter explores how to use Shopify analytics and other tools to track key metrics, understand your store's performance, and make data-driven decisions to optimize and grow your business.

Why Analyze Performance?

- **Identify What's Working:** See which products, marketing campaigns, and strategies are driving the best results.
- **Spot Areas for Improvement:** Uncover weaknesses or bottlenecks hindering your store's performance.
- **Make Informed Decisions:** Base your business decisions on data, not guesswork.
- **Track Progress:** Monitor your store's growth and progress over time.
- **Increase Efficiency:** Optimize your operations and improve efficiency based on data insights.
- **Boost Sales and Profitability:** Ultimately, data-driven analysis can lead to increased sales and profitability.

Shopify Analytics

Shopify provides built-in analytics tools to track various aspects of your store's performance.

- **Dashboard:** The main dashboard provides an overview of key metrics like sales, orders, and visitors.
- **Reports:** Shopify offers various reports to delve deeper into specific areas:
  - **Sales Reports:** Analyze sales by product, channel, time period, etc.
  - **Customer Reports:** Understand customer behavior, demographics, and purchase history.

- o **Marketing Reports:** Track the effectiveness of your marketing campaigns.
- o **Behavior Reports:** Analyze how visitors interact with your website.
- o **Acquisition Reports:** See where your traffic is coming from.
- o **Inventory Reports:** Monitor your inventory levels and product performance.

Key Metrics to Track

Here are some essential metrics to track using Shopify analytics and other tools:

- **Sales and Revenue:**
  - o **Total Sales:** Track your overall sales revenue over time.
  - o **Average Order Value (AOV):** Calculate the average amount customers spend per order.
  - o **Conversion Rate:** Measure the percentage of visitors who make a purchase.
- **Traffic and Engagement:**
  - o **Website Traffic:** Monitor the number of visitors to your store.
  - o **Traffic Sources:** Identify where your traffic is coming from (e.g., search engines, social media, referrals).
  - o **Bounce Rate:** Measure the percentage of visitors who leave your site after viewing only one page.
  - o **Time on Site:** Track how long visitors spend on your website.
  - o **Pages per Session:** Analyze the number of pages visitors view per session.
- **Customer Behavior:**
  - o **Customer Acquisition Cost (CAC):** Calculate the cost of acquiring a new customer.
  - o **Customer Lifetime Value (CLTV):** Estimate the total revenue a customer will generate throughout their relationship with your store.

- o **Repeat Purchase Rate:** Track the percentage of customers who make repeat purchases.
- o **Customer Segmentation:** Analyze customer demographics, purchase history, and behavior to segment your audience.
- **Marketing Performance:**
  - o **Return on Investment (ROI):** Measure the return on your marketing investments.
  - o **Conversion Rate:** Track the percentage of visitors who convert into customers after clicking on your ads or links.
  - o **Cost per Acquisition (CPA):** Calculate the cost of acquiring a customer through a specific marketing channel.

Tools for Performance Analysis

Beyond Shopify analytics, consider these tools:

- **Google Analytics:** Provides in-depth data on website traffic, user behavior, and conversions.
- **Google Search Console:** Offers insights into your website's search performance and indexing status.
- **Hotjar:** Uses heatmaps and recordings to visualize how visitors interact with your website.
- **A/B Testing Tools:** Conduct A/B tests to compare different versions of your website or marketing campaigns.
- **Social Media Analytics:** Track your social media performance and engagement metrics.
- **Email Marketing Analytics:** Monitor email opens, clicks, and conversions.

Optimizing Your Store Based on Data

Here are some ways to use data to optimize your store:

- **Product Optimization:**
  - o **Identify Top-Performing Products:** Focus on promoting and optimizing your best-selling products.

- o **Analyze Product Page Performance:** Identify areas for improvement on your product pages, such as images, descriptions, or calls to action.
- o **Improve Product Recommendations:** Use data to personalize product recommendations and increase cross-selling opportunities.
- **Website Optimization:**
  - o **Improve Website Speed:** Optimize your website's loading speed to enhance user experience and search rankings.
  - o **Enhance Navigation:** Make your website easy to navigate and find products.
  - o **Optimize for Mobile:** Ensure your website is mobile-friendly and provides a seamless experience on all devices.
- **Marketing Optimization:**
  - o **Identify Effective Marketing Channels:** Focus your marketing efforts on the channels that drive the best results.
  - o **Optimize Ad Campaigns:** Use data to improve your ad targeting, creative, and bidding strategies.
  - o **Personalize Marketing Messages:** Segment your audience and tailor your marketing messages to their interests and needs.
- **Customer Experience Optimization:**
  - o **Reduce Cart Abandonment:** Analyze why customers abandon their carts and implement strategies to recover lost sales.
  - o **Improve Customer Service:** Track customer service metrics and identify areas for improvement.
  - o **Increase Customer Lifetime Value:** Implement strategies to encourage repeat purchases and build customer loyalty.

Expanding on Key Concepts

1. Understanding Data Analysis

Data analysis involves collecting, cleaning, and interpreting data to extract meaningful insights. In the context of ecommerce, data analysis can help you understand customer behavior, identify trends, and make informed decisions to improve your store's performance.

2. Types of Data

There are various types of data you can collect and analyze:

- **Quantitative Data:** Numerical data that can be measured and analyzed statistically. (e.g., website traffic, sales revenue, conversion rates)
- **Qualitative Data:** Non-numerical data that provides insights into customer opinions, attitudes, and motivations. (e.g., customer reviews, survey responses, social media comments)

3. Data Visualization

Data visualization involves presenting data in a visual format, such as charts, graphs, and maps. This can make it easier to understand trends and patterns in your data.

4. A/B Testing

A/B testing involves comparing two versions of a webpage, email, or ad to see which performs better. This can help you optimize your store's elements and improve conversion rates.

5. Cohort Analysis

Cohort analysis involves grouping customers based on shared characteristics (e.g., acquisition date, purchase history) and analyzing their behavior over time. This can provide insights into customer lifetime value and identify trends in customer behavior.

6. Predictive Analytics

Predictive analytics uses statistical techniques and machine learning to predict future outcomes based on historical data. This can help you forecast sales, identify potential risks, and make proactive decisions.

7. Data Privacy and Security

When collecting and analyzing customer data, it's crucial to prioritize data privacy and security. Comply with relevant regulations, such as the General Data Protection Regulation (GDPR) and the California Consumer Privacy Act (CCPA).

In Conclusion

Analyzing and improving your store's performance is an ongoing process. By using Shopify analytics, Google Analytics, and other tools, you can track key metrics, understand customer behavior, and make data-driven decisions to optimize your store. Remember to regularly review your data, identify areas for improvement, and implement changes to enhance your website, marketing campaigns, and customer experience. Data-driven optimization is essential for achieving sustainable growth and success in the competitive world of dropshipping.

Chapter 16: Scaling Your Business

You've built a solid foundation for your dropshipping business, and now it's time to scale. This chapter explores strategies to increase sales, expand your operations, and take your business to the next level. We'll cover everything from optimizing your product offerings to exploring new marketing channels and automating your processes.

What Does Scaling Mean?

Scaling means increasing your business's revenue and reach without proportionally increasing your workload or costs. It's about working smarter, not harder, to achieve sustainable growth.

Why Scale Your Dropshipping Business?

- **Increased Revenue and Profit:** Scaling leads to higher sales and profits, allowing you to reinvest in your business and achieve your financial goals.
- **Greater Market Share:** Expanding your reach allows you to capture a larger share of the market and establish your brand as a leader in your niche.
- **Improved Efficiency:** Scaling often involves optimizing your processes and automating tasks, leading to increased efficiency and productivity.
- **Competitive Advantage:** Scaling can give you a competitive edge by allowing you to offer more products, reach more customers, and provide better service.
- **Long-Term Sustainability:** Scaling helps you build a more sustainable business that can withstand market fluctuations and competition.

Strategies for Scaling Your Dropshipping Business

Here are some key strategies to scale your dropshipping operation:

1. Optimize Your Product Offerings

- **Expand Your Product Selection:** Introduce new products that complement your existing offerings and cater to different customer segments.
- **Identify Winning Products:** Analyze your sales data to identify your best-selling products and focus on promoting them.
- **Improve Product Pages:** Optimize your product pages with high-quality images, compelling descriptions, and customer reviews.
- **Offer Product Bundles:** Create product bundles or packages to increase average order value.
- **Introduce Upsells and Cross-sells:** Offer relevant product recommendations to encourage customers to purchase more items.

2. Enhance Your Marketing Efforts

- **Explore New Marketing Channels:** Diversify your marketing efforts by exploring new channels like social media advertising, influencer marketing, or content marketing.
- **Optimize Existing Campaigns:** Analyze the performance of your existing marketing campaigns and make data-driven adjustments to improve their effectiveness.
- **Refine Your Target Audience:** Continuously refine your target audience based on data and customer insights to ensure you're reaching the right people.
- **Improve Your Brand Messaging:** Craft compelling brand messaging that resonates with your target audience and differentiates you from the competition.
- **Build a Strong Brand Identity:** Invest in building a strong brand identity that fosters customer loyalty and recognition.

3. Streamline Your Operations

- **Automate Order Fulfillment:** Use dropshipping apps or integrations to automate order processing and fulfillment.
- **Optimize Shipping and Delivery:** Negotiate with suppliers for faster shipping options or consider using multiple suppliers to reduce delivery times.

- **Implement Inventory Management Systems:** Use inventory management tools to track stock levels and avoid stockouts.
- **Improve Customer Service:** Streamline your customer service processes and provide efficient support through various channels.
- **Outsource Tasks:** Consider outsourcing tasks like customer service, order fulfillment, or marketing to free up your time and focus on strategic growth.

4. Invest in Technology

- **Upgrade Your Shopify Plan:** Consider upgrading to a higher Shopify plan to access more features and resources.
- **Utilize Dropshipping Apps:** Leverage dropshipping apps to automate tasks, enhance functionality, and improve efficiency.
- **Implement Marketing Automation:** Use marketing automation tools to streamline your marketing efforts and personalize customer interactions.
- **Explore Analytics and Reporting Tools:** Invest in analytics and reporting tools to gain deeper insights into your store's performance and make data-driven decisions.

5. Focus on Customer Retention

- **Build a Loyal Customer Base:** Implement strategies to foster customer loyalty and encourage repeat purchases.
- **Offer Excellent Customer Service:** Provide exceptional customer service to build trust and satisfaction.
- **Create a Rewards Program:** Implement a customer rewards program to incentivize repeat business.
- **Personalized Communication:** Send personalized emails and messages to nurture customer relationships.
- **Gather Customer Feedback:** Collect customer feedback through surveys or reviews to understand their needs and preferences.

6. Expand to New Markets

- **Target New Geographic Locations:** Expand your reach by targeting new geographic locations or international markets.
- **Explore New Sales Channels:** Consider selling your products on other platforms like Amazon, eBay, or Etsy.
- **Develop Strategic Partnerships:** Collaborate with other businesses or influencers to reach new audiences.

7. Manage Your Finances Effectively

- **Track Your Expenses:** Monitor your expenses closely to identify areas where you can reduce costs.
- **Optimize Pricing Strategies:** Analyze your pricing strategies to ensure you're maximizing profits without sacrificing competitiveness.
- **Secure Funding:** If needed, explore funding options like loans or investments to fuel your growth.
- **Reinvest Profits:** Reinvest your profits back into your business to support further expansion.

Expanding on Key Concepts

1. Building a Scalable Business Foundation

To successfully scale your dropshipping business, you need a solid foundation:

- **Strong Supplier Relationships:** Establish strong relationships with reliable suppliers who can handle increased order volumes.
- **Efficient Order Fulfillment Process:** Implement an efficient order fulfillment process to ensure timely delivery and customer satisfaction.
- **Excellent Customer Service:** Provide exceptional customer service to build trust and loyalty.
- **Data-Driven Decision Making:** Use data and analytics to track your performance and make informed decisions.

2. Leveraging Automation

Automation is key to scaling your dropshipping business efficiently. Here are some areas where you can automate tasks:

- **Order Processing:** Use dropshipping apps to automatically forward orders to your suppliers.
- **Inventory Management:** Implement inventory management tools to track stock levels and avoid stockouts.
- **Customer Service:** Use chatbots or automated email responses to handle common customer inquiries.
- **Marketing:** Utilize marketing automation tools to schedule social media posts, send email campaigns, and personalize customer interactions.

3. Expanding Your Team

As your business grows, you may need to expand your team to handle increased workload. Here are some roles to consider:

- **Virtual Assistants:** Delegate administrative tasks, customer service, or order processing to virtual assistants.
- **Customer Service Representatives:** Hire dedicated customer service representatives to handle customer inquiries and complaints.
- **Marketing Specialists:** Bring in marketing specialists to manage your social media, email marketing, or paid advertising campaigns.
- **Operations Manager:** Hire an operations manager to oversee your fulfillment process and ensure smooth operations.

4. Managing Inventory and Supply Chain

Scaling your dropshipping business requires careful management of your inventory and supply chain:

- **Multiple Suppliers:** Consider working with multiple suppliers to diversify your product sourcing and reduce the risk of stockouts.
- **Inventory Tracking:** Use inventory management tools to track stock levels and ensure accurate product availability.

- **Supplier Communication:** Maintain clear communication with your suppliers to ensure timely order fulfillment and address any potential issues.
- **Quality Control:** Implement quality control measures to ensure your suppliers consistently deliver high-quality products.

5. International Expansion

Expanding to new international markets can significantly increase your reach and revenue. Here are some considerations:

- **Market Research:** Conduct thorough market research to identify potential target markets and understand their preferences.
- **Localization:** Adapt your website and marketing materials to the local language and culture.
- **Shipping and Logistics:** Research shipping options and logistics for international delivery.
- **Legal and Regulatory Compliance:** Ensure you comply with all relevant legal and regulatory requirements in the target market.

6. Financial Management for Scaling

Effective financial management is crucial for scaling your dropshipping business:

- **Cash Flow Management:** Maintain healthy cash flow to support your growth and cover expenses.
- **Profit Margin Optimization:** Analyze your pricing strategies and negotiate with suppliers to optimize your profit margins.
- **Financial Forecasting:** Develop financial forecasts to anticipate future revenue and expenses.
- **Investment Strategies:** Consider reinvesting your profits or seeking external funding to support your expansion.

In Conclusion

Scaling your dropshipping business requires a strategic approach that involves optimizing your product offerings, enhancing your marketing efforts, streamlining your operations, and investing in technology. By focusing on customer retention, expanding to new markets, and managing your finances effectively, you can achieve sustainable growth and take your business to new heights. Remember to continuously analyze your performance, adapt your strategies, and stay ahead of the curve to thrive in the dynamic world of ecommerce.

Chapter 17: Automation and Tools

In the fast-paced world of dropshipping, efficiency is key. This chapter explores the power of automation and the tools that can streamline your operations, save you time, and ultimately boost your bottom line. We'll delve into various apps and software solutions that can automate tasks, improve productivity, and help you scale your business effectively.

Why Automate Your Dropshipping Business?

- **Save Time and Effort:** Automation takes care of repetitive tasks, freeing up your time to focus on strategic activities that drive growth.
- **Reduce Errors:** Automated processes minimize the risk of human error, ensuring accuracy and consistency in your operations.
- **Improve Efficiency:** Automation streamlines workflows, allowing you to process orders, manage inventory, and handle customer service more efficiently.
- **Increase Productivity:** By automating tasks, you and your team can accomplish more in less time, boosting overall productivity.
- **Scale Your Business:** Automation enables you to handle increased order volumes and expand your operations without adding significant overhead.
- **Improve Customer Satisfaction:** Automated processes can enhance customer satisfaction by providing faster response times, accurate information, and timely delivery.

Types of Automation for Dropshipping

Here are some key areas where automation can transform your dropshipping business:

1. Order Fulfillment

- **Automated Order Processing:** Dropshipping apps like DSers and Oberlo automatically forward orders to your suppliers, eliminating manual data entry and reducing errors.
- **Inventory Management:** Inventory management tools automatically update stock levels, track shipments, and notify you of potential stockouts.
- **Shipping and Tracking:** Shipping automation tools integrate with carriers like USPS, FedEx, and UPS to provide real-time shipping rates, generate labels, and track shipments.

2. Marketing

- **Email Marketing Automation:** Email marketing platforms like Klaviyo and Mailchimp allow you to automate email campaigns, segment your audience, and personalize messages.
- **Social Media Scheduling:** Social media management tools like Buffer and Hootsuite enable you to schedule posts, track mentions, and analyze performance.
- **Chatbots:** Chatbots can automate customer interactions on your website or social media channels, providing instant responses to common inquiries.

3. Customer Service

- **Help Desk Software:** Help desk software like Zendesk and Help Scout automates ticket management, tracks customer interactions, and provides self-service support options.
- **Automated Email Responses:** Set up automated email responses for common inquiries, such as order confirmations, shipping updates, and return requests.
- **Customer Relationship Management (CRM):** CRM systems like HubSpot and Salesforce automate customer data management, track interactions, and personalize communication.

Essential Dropshipping Apps and Tools

Here's a closer look at some popular apps and tools that can automate tasks and improve efficiency in your dropshipping business:

1. DSers

DSers is a powerful dropshipping app that integrates with AliExpress, allowing you to:

- **Automate Order Processing:** Forward orders to suppliers with a single click.
- **Manage Multiple Stores:** Connect and manage multiple Shopify stores from one DSers account.
- **Find Better Suppliers:** Access a supplier directory and find alternative suppliers for your products.
- **Optimize Shipping:** Choose optimal shipping methods and track shipments.
- **Monitor Pricing:** Track product price changes and automatically update your store's pricing.

2. Oberlo

Oberlo is another popular dropshipping app that simplifies product importing and order fulfillment from AliExpress:

- **Product Importing:** Easily import products from AliExpress to your Shopify store.
- **Order Fulfillment:** Automate order processing and fulfillment with a few clicks.
- **Product Customization:** Edit product descriptions, images, and pricing to match your brand.
- **Inventory Management:** Track inventory levels and receive alerts for potential stockouts.
- **ePacket Shipping:** Filter products by ePacket shipping for faster delivery times.

3. Spocket

Spocket focuses on connecting dropshippers with suppliers in the US and EU, offering:

- **Faster Shipping:** Source products from suppliers closer to your customers for faster delivery times.

- **Higher Quality Products:** Access a curated catalog of high-quality products from vetted suppliers.
- **Branded Invoicing:** Add your branding to invoices for a more professional customer experience.
- **Sample Orders:** Order samples to test product quality before listing them on your store.
- **Inventory Management:** Track inventory levels and receive real-time updates.

4. Klaviyo

Klaviyo is a powerful email marketing platform that helps you:

- **Build Email Lists:** Create sign-up forms and landing pages to capture leads.
- **Segment Your Audience:** Segment your email list based on demographics, behavior, and purchase history.
- **Automate Email Campaigns:** Create automated email sequences for welcome emails, abandoned cart recovery, and post-purchase follow-up.
- **Personalize Emails:** Use dynamic content and personalization tokens to tailor emails to individual subscribers.
- **Analyze Performance:** Track email opens, clicks, and conversions to measure campaign effectiveness.

5. Buffer

Buffer is a social media management tool that allows you to:

- **Schedule Posts:** Schedule social media posts in advance across multiple platforms.
- **Track Mentions:** Monitor mentions of your brand or products on social media.
- **Analyze Performance:** Track your social media performance and engagement metrics.
- **Collaborate with Team Members:** Manage social media accounts with multiple team members.
- **Analyze Competitors:** Track your competitors' social media activity and performance.

6. Zendesk

Zendesk is a popular help desk software that helps you:

- **Manage Customer Inquiries:** Track customer inquiries, manage tickets, and provide support through various channels.
- **Automate Responses:** Set up automated email responses for common inquiries.
- **Create a Knowledge Base:** Build a knowledge base or FAQ section for self-service support.
- **Analyze Performance:** Track customer service metrics and identify areas for improvement.
- **Integrate with Other Tools:** Integrate with other tools like Shopify, Salesforce, and Slack.

Expanding on Key Concepts

1. Identifying Tasks to Automate

To effectively automate your dropshipping business, start by identifying tasks that are:

- **Repetitive:** Tasks that are performed frequently and follow a predictable pattern.
- **Time-Consuming:** Tasks that take up a significant amount of your time.
- **Prone to Errors:** Tasks that are susceptible to human error.
- **Data-Driven:** Tasks that involve processing or analyzing data.
- **Customer-Facing:** Tasks that involve interacting with customers.

By automating these types of tasks, you can free up your time, reduce errors, and improve efficiency.

2. Choosing the Right Automation Tools

When selecting automation tools, consider these factors:

- **Features:** Does the tool offer the features you need to automate your specific tasks?
- **Ease of Use:** Is the tool user-friendly and easy to integrate with your existing systems?
- **Pricing:** Does the tool's pricing fit your budget and business needs?
- **Support:** Does the tool provider offer adequate support and resources?
- **Scalability:** Can the tool scale with your business as your needs grow?
- **Integrations:** Does the tool integrate with other tools and platforms you use?

3. Implementing Automation Effectively

Here are some tips for implementing automation effectively:

- **Start Small:** Begin by automating a few key tasks and gradually expand your automation efforts.
- **Document Your Processes:** Clearly document your processes before automating them to ensure smooth implementation.
- **Test Thoroughly:** Test your automated workflows thoroughly to identify and address any potential issues.
- **Monitor Performance:** Track the performance of your automated processes and make adjustments as needed.
- **Train Your Team:** Provide training to your team on how to use the automation tools and processes.

4. The Role of Artificial Intelligence (AI)

Artificial intelligence (AI) is playing an increasingly important role in automation. AI-powered tools can:

- **Personalize Customer Experiences:** Analyze customer data to provide personalized product recommendations and marketing messages.
- **Automate Customer Service:** Use chatbots to answer customer inquiries and resolve issues.

- **Optimize Marketing Campaigns:** Analyze data to optimize ad targeting, bidding strategies, and content personalization.
- **Improve Fraud Detection:** Identify and prevent fraudulent activities.
- **Enhance Product Recommendations:** Use machine learning to suggest relevant products to customers.

5. The Future of Automation in Dropshipping

Automation will continue to play a crucial role in the future of dropshipping. Here are some trends to watch:

- **Increased AI Adoption:** More dropshipping businesses will adopt AI-powered tools to automate tasks and improve efficiency.
- **Hyper-Personalization:** Automation will enable hyper-personalization of customer experiences, tailoring product recommendations, marketing messages, and customer service interactions to individual preferences.
- **Predictive Analytics:** Predictive analytics will help dropshippers anticipate customer needs, optimize inventory management, and make proactive decisions.
- **Autonomous Order Fulfillment:** Advancements in automation may lead to fully autonomous order fulfillment processes, further streamlining operations.

In Conclusion

Automation is essential for dropshipping businesses to save time, reduce errors, improve efficiency, and scale effectively. By leveraging apps and software solutions, you can automate tasks like order fulfillment, marketing, and customer service. Remember to choose the right tools, implement automation strategically, and stay informed about the latest advancements in AI and automation to stay ahead of the curve and maximize your business's potential.

Part 5: Beyond the Basics

Chapter 18: Building a Brand

In the competitive world of dropshipping, building a strong brand is essential for standing out and achieving long-term success. This chapter explores the key elements of brand building, from defining your brand identity to fostering customer loyalty. We'll delve into strategies for creating a memorable brand that resonates with your target audience and drives sustainable growth.

What is a Brand?

A brand is more than just a logo or a name. It's the overall perception that customers have of your business. It encompasses your values, personality, messaging, and customer experience. A strong brand creates an emotional connection with customers, fostering trust, loyalty, and advocacy.

Why Brand Building Matters for Dropshipping

- **Differentiation:** In a crowded market, a strong brand helps you differentiate yourself from the competition.
- **Customer Loyalty:** A strong brand fosters customer loyalty, encouraging repeat purchases and positive word-of-mouth marketing.
- **Premium Pricing:** Customers are often willing to pay more for products from brands they trust and admire.
- **Brand Recognition:** A recognizable brand makes it easier for customers to identify and remember your business.
- **Marketing Effectiveness:** A strong brand amplifies your marketing efforts by creating a consistent and memorable message.
- **Business Value:** A strong brand adds value to your business, making it more attractive to investors or potential buyers.

Creating a Strong Brand Identity

Building a strong brand starts with defining your brand identity. This involves:

1. Define Your Brand Values

Your brand values are the core principles that guide your business decisions and actions. They should reflect your company's mission and beliefs. Examples of brand values include:

- **Quality:** Commitment to providing high-quality products or services.
- **Innovation:** Focus on creativity and innovation.
- **Sustainability:** Dedication to environmental and social responsibility.
- **Customer Focus:** Prioritizing customer satisfaction and experience.
- **Trust and Transparency:** Building trust with customers through transparency and honesty.

2. Determine Your Brand Personality

Your brand personality is the human-like characteristics associated with your brand. It helps customers connect with your brand on an emotional level. Consider these dimensions:

- **Excitement:** Bold, spirited, imaginative.
- **Sincerity:** Down-to-earth, honest, wholesome.
- **Competence:** Reliable, intelligent, successful.
- **Sophistication:** Upper class, charming.
- **Ruggedness:** Outdoorsy, tough.

3. Craft Your Brand Story

Your brand story is the narrative that explains your brand's origins, values, and mission. It helps customers understand who you are and what you stand for. A compelling brand story can create an emotional connection and build trust.

4. Develop Your Brand Messaging

Your brand messaging is the way you communicate your brand's value proposition and personality to your audience. It should be consistent across all your marketing channels. Consider:

- **Tagline:** A short, memorable phrase that captures your brand essence.
- **Value Proposition:** A clear statement of the benefits your brand offers to customers.
- **Brand Voice:** The tone and style of your communication, reflecting your brand personality.

5. Design Your Visual Identity

Your visual identity is the visual representation of your brand. It includes:

- **Logo:** A visual symbol that represents your brand.
- **Color Palette:** The colors associated with your brand.
- **Typography:** The fonts used in your branding and marketing materials.
- **Imagery:** The types of images and visuals used to represent your brand.

Fostering Customer Loyalty

Building a strong brand is not just about creating a compelling identity. It's also about fostering customer loyalty and advocacy. Here are some strategies:

1. Provide Excellent Customer Service

Exceptional customer service is crucial for building trust and loyalty. Respond to inquiries promptly, resolve issues efficiently, and go the extra mile to exceed customer expectations.

2. Create a Positive Customer Experience

Make every interaction with your brand a positive one. This includes providing a user-friendly website, offering high-quality products, and ensuring smooth order fulfillment and delivery.

3. Build a Community

Create a sense of community around your brand by engaging with customers on social media, hosting events, or creating online forums.

4. Offer Exclusive Benefits

Reward loyal customers with exclusive benefits like discounts, early access to new products, or personalized offers.

5. Seek Customer Feedback

Actively seek customer feedback through surveys, reviews, or social media interactions. Use this feedback to improve your products, services, and customer experience.

6. Show Appreciation

Show your appreciation for your customers by thanking them for their business, sending birthday messages, or offering personalized gifts.

7. Be Consistent

Consistency is key to building a strong brand. Maintain a consistent brand identity, messaging, and customer experience across all your touchpoints.

Expanding on Key Concepts

1. The Importance of Brand Storytelling

Brand storytelling is a powerful tool for connecting with customers on an emotional level. Here are some tips for effective brand storytelling:

- **Be Authentic:** Share your genuine story and values.
- **Focus on Emotion:** Connect with your audience through emotions like empathy, inspiration, or humor.
- **Keep it Concise:** Tell your story in a clear and concise way.

- **Use Visuals:** Enhance your story with compelling visuals.
- **Be Consistent:** Integrate your brand story into all your marketing efforts.

2. Building a Brand Community

Creating a brand community fosters customer loyalty and advocacy. Here are some ways to build a community:

- **Social Media Engagement:** Interact with your audience on social media, respond to comments, and participate in conversations.
- **Online Forums:** Create online forums or groups where customers can connect with each other and your brand.
- **Events and Meetups:** Host events or meetups to bring your customers together in person.
- **User-Generated Content:** Encourage customers to create and share content related to your brand.
- **Brand Ambassadors:** Identify and partner with loyal customers who can act as brand ambassadors.

3. Measuring Brand Performance

Tracking your brand performance is essential for understanding how your brand is perceived and making adjustments to your strategy. Here are some key metrics to track:

- **Brand Awareness:** Measure brand awareness through surveys, social media mentions, or website traffic.
- **Customer Satisfaction:** Track customer satisfaction through surveys, reviews, or feedback forms.
- **Customer Loyalty:** Measure customer loyalty through repeat purchase rate, customer lifetime value, or Net Promoter Score (NPS).
- **Social Media Engagement:** Monitor social media engagement metrics like likes, comments, and shares.
- **Website Traffic:** Track website traffic from branded search terms.

4. Brand Protection

Protecting your brand is crucial for maintaining its integrity and value. Here are some ways to protect your brand:

- **Trademark Registration:** Register your brand name and logo as trademarks to protect them from infringement.
- **Monitor Brand Mentions:** Use social listening tools to monitor mentions of your brand and address any negative feedback or misuse.
- **Enforce Brand Guidelines:** Ensure consistent use of your brand identity and messaging across all your marketing materials.
- **Address Counterfeit Products:** Take action to address any counterfeit products that may damage your brand reputation.

5. The Role of Brand in Dropshipping

Building a strong brand is particularly important in dropshipping, where you may be selling products from multiple suppliers. A strong brand can help you:

- **Create a Unique Identity:** Differentiate yourself from other dropshippers selling similar products.
- **Build Trust with Customers:** Establish trust with customers who may be hesitant to purchase from an unknown online store.
- **Increase Customer Lifetime Value:** Foster customer loyalty and encourage repeat purchases.
- **Charge Premium Prices:** Command higher prices for your products based on the perceived value of your brand.

In Conclusion

Building a strong brand is a crucial investment for dropshipping success. By defining your brand identity, crafting a compelling brand story, and fostering customer loyalty, you can create a memorable brand that resonates with your target audience and drives sustainable growth. Remember to be consistent, track your brand performance, and protect your brand's integrity to establish a strong presence in the competitive ecommerce landscape.

Chapter 19: Long-Term Strategies

Building a successful dropshipping business isn't a sprint; it's a marathon. This chapter focuses on developing long-term strategies for sustainable growth and adapting to the ever-changing ecommerce landscape. We'll explore how to anticipate trends, build resilience, and position your business for continued success in the years to come.

Why Long-Term Strategies Matter

- **Sustainable Growth:** Long-term strategies focus on building a business that can thrive over time, not just achieve short-term gains.
- **Adaptability:** The ecommerce landscape is constantly evolving. Long-term strategies help you adapt to changes and stay ahead of the curve.
- **Competitive Advantage:** A long-term perspective allows you to build a stronger brand, cultivate customer loyalty, and establish a sustainable competitive advantage.
- **Resilience:** Long-term strategies help you build a more resilient business that can withstand market fluctuations and challenges.
- **Financial Stability:** Planning for the long term helps you achieve financial stability and avoid short-term pitfalls.

Key Elements of Long-Term Strategies

1. Vision and Mission

- **Define Your Vision:** Create a clear vision for your business's future, outlining your long-term goals and aspirations.
- **Craft Your Mission Statement:** Develop a concise mission statement that defines your business's purpose and how you will achieve your vision.

2. Market Analysis and Forecasting

- **Monitor Industry Trends:** Stay informed about industry trends, emerging technologies, and changing consumer behavior.
- **Analyze Competitor Strategies:** Keep an eye on your competitors' actions and adapt your strategies accordingly.
- **Forecast Market Demand:** Anticipate future market demand and adjust your product offerings and marketing efforts accordingly.

3. Product Development and Innovation

- **Expand Your Product Line:** Continuously introduce new products that complement your existing offerings and cater to evolving customer needs.
- **Improve Existing Products:** Gather customer feedback and make improvements to your existing products to enhance their value and appeal.
- **Explore New Product Categories:** Consider expanding into new product categories that align with your brand and target audience.
- **Invest in Research and Development:** Allocate resources to research and development to stay ahead of the curve and innovate in your niche.

4. Customer Relationship Management (CRM)

- **Build Customer Loyalty:** Implement strategies to foster customer loyalty and encourage repeat purchases.
- **Personalize Customer Interactions:** Use data and automation to personalize customer interactions and provide tailored experiences.
- **Gather Customer Feedback:** Actively seek customer feedback to understand their needs and preferences.
- **Develop a Customer-Centric Culture:** Prioritize customer satisfaction and build a culture that values customer relationships.

5. Operational Efficiency

- **Streamline Your Processes:** Continuously optimize your operations to improve efficiency and reduce costs.
- **Invest in Automation:** Leverage automation tools to automate tasks and free up your time for strategic activities.
- **Outsource Non-Core Functions:** Consider outsourcing tasks like customer service, order fulfillment, or marketing to specialized providers.
- **Build a Strong Team:** Hire and train a skilled team that can support your long-term growth.

6. Financial Planning

- **Develop a Long-Term Financial Plan:** Create a financial plan that outlines your revenue projections, expenses, and investment strategies.
- **Secure Funding:** If needed, explore funding options like loans or investments to support your long-term growth.
- **Manage Cash Flow:** Maintain healthy cash flow to ensure you can cover expenses and reinvest in your business.
- **Diversify Revenue Streams:** Explore new revenue streams or business models to reduce reliance on a single source of income.

7. Adaptability and Resilience

- **Embrace Change:** Be prepared to adapt to changes in the market, technology, and consumer behavior.
- **Build a Flexible Business Model:** Create a business model that can adapt to changing circumstances and market conditions.
- **Develop Contingency Plans:** Anticipate potential challenges and develop contingency plans to mitigate risks.
- **Learn from Mistakes:** Embrace a culture of learning and continuous improvement, using mistakes as opportunities to grow and adapt.

Expanding on Key Concepts

1. The Importance of Market Research

Continuous market research is essential for long-term success. Here are some key areas to focus on:

- **Industry Trends:** Stay informed about the latest trends, emerging technologies, and changing consumer preferences in your industry.
- **Competitor Analysis:** Monitor your competitors' actions, strategies, and product offerings to identify opportunities and threats.
- **Customer Insights:** Gather data and insights about your target audience, including their demographics, needs, and pain points.
- **Market Segmentation:** Segment your market to identify specific customer groups and tailor your offerings and marketing messages accordingly.

2. Building a Sustainable Competitive Advantage

A sustainable competitive advantage is something that sets your business apart from the competition and is difficult to replicate. Here are some ways to build a sustainable competitive advantage:

- **Strong Brand Identity:** Create a unique and memorable brand that resonates with your target audience.
- **Exceptional Customer Experience:** Provide outstanding customer service and create a positive customer experience that fosters loyalty.
- **Product Differentiation:** Offer unique products or features that differentiate you from the competition.
- **Operational Efficiency:** Streamline your operations and reduce costs to offer competitive pricing.
- **Innovation:** Continuously innovate and introduce new products or services to stay ahead of the curve.

3. Embracing Technology

Technology plays a crucial role in long-term growth and adaptability. Here are some ways to leverage technology:

- **Ecommerce Platform:** Choose a robust ecommerce platform like Shopify that can scale with your business and offer the features you need.
- **Automation Tools:** Utilize automation tools to streamline your operations, marketing efforts, and customer service.
- **Data Analytics:** Leverage data analytics to track your performance, understand customer behavior, and make informed decisions.
- **Artificial Intelligence (AI):** Explore AI-powered tools to personalize customer experiences, optimize marketing campaigns, and improve efficiency.

4. Building a Strong Team

Your team is your most valuable asset. Here are some tips for building a strong team:

- **Hire the Right People:** Recruit talented individuals who align with your company culture and values.
- **Provide Training and Development:** Invest in training and development to empower your team and help them grow.
- **Foster a Positive Work Environment:** Create a positive and supportive work environment that encourages collaboration and innovation.
- **Delegate Effectively:** Delegate tasks effectively to empower your team and free up your time for strategic activities.

5. Adapting to Market Changes

The ecommerce landscape is constantly evolving. Here are some ways to adapt to market changes:

- **Monitor Trends:** Stay informed about industry trends, emerging technologies, and changing consumer behavior.
- **Be Flexible:** Be willing to adjust your strategies and adapt your business model as needed.
- **Embrace Innovation:** Continuously innovate and introduce new products or services to stay ahead of the curve.
- **Seek Customer Feedback:** Actively seek customer feedback to understand their evolving needs and preferences.

6. Building a Sustainable Business

Sustainability is becoming increasingly important for businesses. Here are some ways to build a more sustainable dropshipping business:

- **Ethical Sourcing:** Source products from suppliers who adhere to ethical and sustainable practices.
- **Eco-Friendly Packaging:** Use eco-friendly packaging materials to reduce your environmental impact.
- **Reduce Waste:** Implement strategies to reduce waste in your operations and supply chain.
- **Support Social Causes:** Partner with charities or non-profit organizations to support social causes that align with your brand values.

In Conclusion

Developing long-term strategies is essential for achieving sustainable growth and adapting to the ever-changing ecommerce landscape. By defining your vision, analyzing the market, innovating your product offerings, and building a strong brand, you can position your dropshipping business for continued success. Remember to prioritize customer relationships, optimize your operations, and embrace technology to stay ahead of the curve and build a resilient and thriving business.

Chapter 20: Common Mistakes to Avoid

Dropshipping can be a rewarding venture, but it's not without its challenges. This chapter highlights common pitfalls that new dropshippers often encounter. By understanding these mistakes and learning how to avoid them, you can increase your chances of success and build a thriving dropshipping business.

1. Poor Niche Selection

Choosing the right niche is crucial for dropshipping success. Avoid these common niche-related mistakes:

- **Choosing a Niche That's Too Broad:** Broad niches have high competition, making it difficult to stand out and attract customers. Instead, focus on a specific sub-niche with less competition.
    - **Example:** Instead of "fashion accessories," consider "handmade leather bracelets for men" or "eco-friendly yoga apparel."
- **Choosing a Niche with No Demand:** If there's little demand for the products in your niche, you'll struggle to generate sales. Conduct thorough market research to validate your niche idea before investing time and resources.
    - **Example:** Avoid niches with low search volume or limited customer interest on social media or online forums.
- **Ignoring Shipping Costs:** High shipping costs can significantly impact your profit margins and make your products less competitive. Factor in shipping costs when evaluating the profitability of a niche.
    - **Example:** Consider the product's weight, dimensions, and origin when assessing shipping costs. Look for suppliers who offer competitive shipping rates or consider sourcing products from locations closer to your target market.

- **Overlooking Legal and Regulatory Requirements:** Failing to comply with legal requirements can lead to fines, penalties, or even business closure. Research any legal or regulatory requirements that may apply to your niche, such as product safety standards, licensing requirements, or import/export regulations.
  - o **Example:** If you're selling products that require specific certifications or licenses, ensure your suppliers comply with those regulations.

2. Neglecting Product Research

Choosing the right products is essential for dropshipping success. Avoid these product research mistakes:

- **Focusing Only on Trending Products:** While trending products can be profitable, they may also be short-lived fads. Focus on products with long-term potential and consider seasonality and market trends.
  - o **Example:** Instead of solely relying on trending product lists, analyze customer reviews, identify product gaps, and research emerging technologies to find products with lasting appeal.
- **Ignoring Product Quality:** Poor product quality can lead to customer complaints, returns, and damage to your brand reputation. Order samples from potential suppliers to assess product quality firsthand and read customer reviews carefully.
  - o **Example:** Don't solely rely on product images or descriptions. Request samples to evaluate the product's materials, construction, and functionality.
- **Overlooking Shipping Times:** Long shipping times can frustrate customers and lead to negative reviews. Choose suppliers who offer fast and reliable shipping options, ideally with tracking information.
  - o **Example:** Consider using suppliers located closer to your target market or offering expedited shipping options to reduce delivery times.
- **Not Calculating Profit Margins Accurately:** Failing to calculate profit margins accurately can lead to financial

losses. Factor in all costs, including product cost, shipping costs, marketing expenses, and platform fees, when determining your pricing strategy.

- o **Example:** Use a spreadsheet or profit margin calculator to accurately calculate your profit margins for each product. Consider offering volume discounts or bundling products to increase profitability.

3. Underestimating Supplier Importance

Your suppliers are your partners in delivering products and customer satisfaction. Avoid these supplier-related mistakes:

- **Relying on a Single Supplier:** Relying on a single supplier can be risky. If your supplier experiences issues, your business can be disrupted. Diversify your supplier base to mitigate risks.
  - o **Example:** Work with multiple suppliers for the same or similar products to ensure you have backup options in case of stockouts, delays, or supplier issues.
- **Not Vetting Suppliers Thoroughly:** Working with unreliable suppliers can lead to product quality issues, shipping delays, and poor customer service. Thoroughly vet potential suppliers before partnering with them.
  - o **Example:** Check supplier ratings and reviews, order samples, and communicate with them directly to assess their reliability, responsiveness, and product quality.
- **Ignoring Supplier Communication:** Poor communication with suppliers can lead to misunderstandings, errors, and delays. Establish clear communication channels and expectations with your suppliers.
  - o **Example:** Use email, messaging apps, or project management tools to communicate with your suppliers effectively. Clarify expectations regarding order processing, shipping times, and customer service.
- **Not Negotiating with Suppliers:** As your business grows, negotiate with your suppliers for better terms, such as volume

discounts, faster shipping options, or custom branding options.

- o **Example:** Don't be afraid to ask for discounts or negotiate terms that benefit both you and your supplier. Building strong relationships with your suppliers can lead to more favorable terms.

4. Neglecting Website Optimization

Your website is your online storefront. Avoid these website optimization mistakes:

- **Poor Website Design:** A poorly designed website can deter customers and create a negative impression of your brand. Invest in a professional-looking website with a user-friendly interface and clear navigation.
  - o **Example:** Choose a visually appealing Shopify theme that aligns with your brand and niche. Ensure your website is mobile-responsive and easy to navigate on all devices.
- **Slow Loading Speed:** A slow website can frustrate customers and lead to higher bounce rates. Optimize your website's loading speed by compressing images, minimizing code, and using a content delivery network (CDN).
  - o **Example:** Use tools like Google PageSpeed Insights or GTmetrix to analyze your website's loading speed and identify areas for improvement.
- **Lack of Mobile Optimization:** With the majority of online traffic coming from mobile devices, neglecting mobile optimization can significantly impact your sales. Ensure your website is mobile-friendly and provides a seamless experience on all devices.
  - o **Example:** Choose a mobile-responsive theme, optimize images for mobile, and simplify your website's navigation for smaller screens.
- **Poor Product Pages:** Unattractive or poorly optimized product pages can discourage customers from making a purchase. Use high-quality images, compelling descriptions, and customer reviews to enhance your product pages.

o **Example:** Showcase your products from multiple angles, highlight key features and benefits, and include customer testimonials to build trust and encourage conversions.

5. Ineffective Marketing

Marketing is essential for driving traffic and generating sales. Avoid these marketing mistakes:

- **Relying Solely on Paid Advertising:** While paid advertising can be effective, it can also be expensive. Diversify your marketing efforts by exploring other channels like SEO, social media marketing, and content marketing.
  - o **Example:** Invest in SEO to attract organic traffic, build a strong social media presence, and create valuable content that engages your audience and drives traffic to your store.
- **Ignoring Social Media:** Social media is a powerful tool for reaching your target audience and building brand awareness. Create a strong social media presence and engage with your audience regularly.
  - o **Example:** Choose the social media platforms that align with your target audience and create engaging content that showcases your products and brand personality.
- **Neglecting Email Marketing:** Email marketing is a valuable channel for nurturing customer relationships and promoting your products. Build an email list and create effective email campaigns.
  - o **Example:** Offer incentives to encourage email sign-ups, segment your audience, and send personalized emails to promote your products and offers.
- **Not Tracking Marketing Performance:** Failing to track your marketing performance can lead to wasted resources and missed opportunities. Use analytics tools to track your marketing campaigns and measure their effectiveness.
  - o **Example:** Track key metrics like website traffic, conversion rates, and return on investment (ROI) to

understand which marketing channels and strategies are driving the best results.

6. Poor Customer Service

Customer service is crucial for building trust and loyalty. Avoid these customer service mistakes:

- **Slow Response Times:** Slow response times can frustrate customers and damage your brand reputation. Respond to customer inquiries promptly, ideally within 24 hours.
    - o **Example:** Use help desk software or live chat to manage customer inquiries efficiently and provide timely responses.
- **Unhelpful or Unprofessional Communication:** Unhelpful or unprofessional communication can create a negative customer experience. Be polite, helpful, and solutions-oriented in all your customer interactions.
    - o **Example:** Train your customer service team to handle inquiries effectively and provide accurate information. Use a professional tone and avoid using jargon or technical terms.
- **Lack of a Clear Return Policy:** A confusing or restrictive return policy can deter customers and lead to negative reviews. Create a clear and customer-friendly return policy that outlines the process for returns and refunds.
    - o **Example:** Clearly state your return and refund policy on your website and in your order confirmation emails. Make the return process as easy as possible for customers.
- **Ignoring Customer Feedback:** Customer feedback is valuable for improving your products, services, and customer experience. Actively seek customer feedback and use it to make improvements.
    - o **Example:** Encourage customers to leave reviews, send surveys, or use social listening tools to gather feedback and identify areas for improvement.

7. Lack of Planning and Organization

Running a successful dropshipping business requires planning and organization. Avoid these mistakes:

- **Not Having a Business Plan:** A business plan outlines your business goals, strategies, and financial projections. It serves as a roadmap for your business.
    - **Example:** Create a business plan that includes your target market, product offerings, marketing plan, financial projections, and operational plan.
- **Poor Inventory Management:** Poor inventory management can lead to stockouts, delays, and frustrated customers. Use inventory management tools to track stock levels and ensure accurate product availability.
    - **Example:** Integrate your store with inventory management apps that automatically update stock levels and provide alerts for potential stockouts.
- **Not Tracking Finances:** Failing to track your finances can lead to financial mismanagement and missed opportunities. Use accounting software or hire a bookkeeper to track your income and expenses.
    - **Example:** Track your sales, expenses, and profits regularly. Use this information to make informed decisions about your pricing, marketing, and operations.
- **Not Setting Goals:** Setting clear goals helps you stay focused and motivated. Set specific, measurable, achievable, relevant, and time-bound (SMART) goals for your business.
    - **Example:** Set goals for your sales, website traffic, customer acquisition, and other key metrics. Track your progress and make adjustments to your strategies as needed.

8. Legal and Ethical Issues

Operating a legitimate and ethical business is crucial for long-term success. Avoid these legal and ethical mistakes:

- **Ignoring Copyright and Trademark Laws:** Using copyrighted or trademarked materials without permission can lead to legal issues. Ensure you have the right to use any images, logos, or content you use on your website or in your marketing materials.

- o **Example:** Use royalty-free images or obtain licenses for any copyrighted materials you use. Avoid using logos or brand names that are trademarked by others.
- **Not Complying with Data Privacy Regulations:** Protect customer data and comply with data privacy regulations like the General Data Protection Regulation (GDPR) and the California Consumer Privacy Act (CCPA).
  - o **Example:** Implement a clear privacy policy that outlines how you collect, use, and protect customer data. Obtain consent before collecting any personal information.
- **Selling Counterfeit Products:** Selling counterfeit products is illegal and can damage your brand reputation. Ensure your suppliers are authorized to sell the products they offer and that the products are genuine.
  - o **Example:** Thoroughly vet your suppliers and verify the authenticity of their products. Avoid selling products that infringe on intellectual property rights.
- **Misrepresenting Products or Services:** Misrepresenting your products or services can mislead customers and damage your brand reputation. Be honest and transparent in your marketing and product descriptions.
  - o **Example:** Accurately describe your products and their features. Avoid making false or misleading claims about your products or services.

9. Giving Up Too Soon

Building a successful dropshipping business takes time and effort. Avoid giving up too soon.

- **Be Patient:** Don't expect overnight success. Building a profitable dropshipping business takes time, patience, and persistence.
  - o **Example:** Focus on building a strong foundation, creating a unique brand, and providing excellent customer service. Don't get discouraged by initial setbacks or slow progress.

- **Learn from Mistakes:** Everyone makes mistakes. Use your mistakes as learning opportunities and adjust your strategies accordingly.
  - ○ **Example:** Analyze your performance data, identify areas for improvement, and implement changes to your website, marketing, or operations.
- **Stay Motivated:** Running a business can be challenging. Stay motivated by setting goals, celebrating your achievements, and connecting with other entrepreneurs.
  - ○ **Example:** Join online communities or forums for dropshippers to connect with other entrepreneurs, share experiences, and learn from each other.
- **Seek Support:** Don't be afraid to ask for help or seek support from mentors, coaches, or online communities.
  - ○ **Example:** Connect with experienced dropshippers, join online courses or workshops, or hire a business coach to guide you through the challenges of building a dropshipping business.

In Conclusion

Dropshipping can be a rewarding venture, but it's important to be aware of common pitfalls that new entrepreneurs often encounter. By avoiding these mistakes, you can increase your chances of success and build a thriving dropshipping business. Remember to choose the right niche, conduct thorough product research, work with reliable suppliers, optimize your website, implement effective marketing strategies, provide excellent customer service, and stay persistent in your pursuit of success.

ABOUT THE AUTHOR

Gabriel Mensah is a passionate advocate for personal growth and transformation. With over 30 years of experience in copywriting, I have honed a deep understanding of human behavior and the power of words to inspire and motivate. I am a firm believer that lasting change is possible for anyone willing to embrace the process of habit formation.

Through my writing, I seek to empower individuals to unlock their full potential, achieve their goals, and create a life of purpose and fulfillment. I am committed to providing practical, actionable strategies that readers can implement in their daily lives.

When not writing, I enjoy spending time in nature, exploring new cultures, practicing yoga, or engaging in creative pursuits. I am also an avid reader and lifelong learner, constantly seeking new knowledge and insights to share with others.

Printed in Great Britain
by Amazon

57246173R00079